Cambridge Elements ≡

Elements in Translation and Interpreting
edited by
Kirsten Malmkjær
University of Leicester

T0287039

TRANSLATION
IN ANALYTIC PHILOSOPHY

Francesca Ervas
University of Cagliari

CAMBRIDGE
UNIVERSITY PRESS

Shaftesbury Road, Cambridge CB2 8EA, United Kingdom

One Liberty Plaza, 20th Floor, New York, NY 10006, USA

477 Williamstown Road, Port Melbourne, VIC 3207, Australia

314–321, 3rd Floor, Plot 3, Splendor Forum, Jasola District Centre,
New Delhi – 110025, India

103 Penang Road, #05–06/07, Visioncrest Commercial, Singapore 238467

Cambridge University Press is part of Cambridge University Press & Assessment,
a department of the University of Cambridge.

We share the University's mission to contribute to society through the pursuit of
education, learning and research at the highest international levels of excellence.

www.cambridge.org
Information on this title: www.cambridge.org/9781009454292

DOI: 10.1017/9781009351294

First published 2023

A catalogue record for this publication is available from the British Library

ISBN 978-1-009-45429-2 Hardback
ISBN 978-1-009-35132-4 Paperback
ISSN 2633-6480 (online)
ISSN 2633-6472 (print)

Cambridge University Press & Assessment has no responsibility for the persistence
or accuracy of URLs for external or third-party internet websites referred to in this
publication and does not guarantee that any content on such websites is, or will
remain, accurate or appropriate.

Translation in Analytic Philosophy

Elements in Translation and Interpreting

DOI: 10.1017/9781009351294
First published online: December 2023

Francesca Ervas
University of Cagliari

Author for correspondence: Francesca Ervas, ervas@unica.it

Abstract: This Element aims to introduce the different definitions of translation provided in the history of analytic philosophy. Starting from the definitions of translation as paraphrase, calculus, and language games, the Element explores the main philosophical-analytic notions used to explain translation from Frege and Wittgenstein onwards. Particular attention is paid to the concept of translation equivalence in the work of Quine, Davidson, and Sellars, and to the problem of translating implicit versus explicit meaning into another language as discussed by Grice, Kripke, and the contemporary trends in analytic philosophy of language.

Keywords: translation, analytic philosophy, philosophy of language, translation equivalence, translatability

ISBNs: 9781009454292 (HB), 9781009351324 (PB), 9781009351294 (OC)
ISSNs: 2633-6480 (online), 2633-6472 (print)

Contents

Introduction

This Element draws on, and from, work on translation equivalence and translation definition in analytic philosophy that I have published over the past fifteen years in a series of papers in philosophy and linguistics journals. The purpose of this Element is to present various interpretations of translation as observed in the history of analytic philosophy, showing their theoretical limitations as well as their conceptual value for translation theory. It begins with examining the definitions of translation as paraphrase, calculus, and language game, and then delves into the key philosophical-analytic concepts used to describe translation.

Analytic philosophy is a philosophical approach that emphasizes the use of logical analysis and empirical methods in the pursuit of understanding and solving philosophical problems. It emerged in the early twentieth century in 'continental' Europe[1] and is characterized by its focus on clarity, precision, and argumentative rigour, as well as its rejection of traditional metaphysical and speculative approaches to philosophy. Analytic philosophers typically seek to clarify concepts, examine the logical relationships between propositions, and use scientific methods to evaluate philosophical claims (Glock, 2008). In analytic philosophy of language, the problem of meaning has been central to philosophical debates. In such a framework, the concept of translation has proved to be pivotal in answering the question of the nature of meaning and analysing the problem of meaning sameness across linguistic differences (Malmkjær, 1998).

Willard van Orman Quine, one of the most prominent analytic philosophers and well-known scholars in the interdisciplinary field of Translation Studies (Van Leuven-Zwart & Naaijkens, 1991), attempts to understand the problem of meaning by studying the problem of translation. He defines meaning itself, in the second chapter of *Word and Object* (1960), as 'what a sentence shares with its translation' (Quine, 1960: 32). Quine's analysis aims to determine what 'same in meaning' means and what this commonality between a sentence and its translation might be. The central problem of Quinean philosophy, which is also taken up by Donald Davidson, is to describe what 'the same meaning' is. This problem pertains to all types of translation, not just *interlingual* translation (between different languages) but also *intralingual* translation (within the same language) or *rewording* (cf. Jakobson, 1959). Even when we communicate with

---

[1] Analytic philosophy has been opposed to 'continental' philosophy (see, for example, D'Agostini, 1997), wrongly confronting the philosophical style of some philosophers ('analytic') with the geographical area of other philosophers ('continental'). However, many philosophers considered that father founders of analytic philosophy, such as Frege, Carnap, and Wittgenstein, came from 'continental' Europe (see Section 1 and 2).

someone who speaks our language, we may wonder what ensures that they understand us in the same way that we intend:

> On deeper reflection, radical translation begins at home. Must we equate our neighbour's English words with the same strings of phonemes in our own mouths? Certainly not; for sometimes we do not thus equate them. Sometimes we find it to be in the interest of communication to recognize that our neighbour's use of some word, such as 'cool' or 'square' or 'hopefully', differs from ours, and so we *translate that word of his* into a different string of phonemes in our idiolect. (Quine, 1969a: 46, italics added)

In the same vein, Davidson remarked that comprehending another person always entails reflecting on what it means 'to assign the same meaning to the words', whether they speak our mother tongue or a language we are unfamiliar with:

> The problem of interpretation is *domestic* as well as *foreign*: it surfaces for speakers of the *same language* in the form of the question, how can it be determined that the language is the *same*? Speakers of the *same* language can go on the assumption that for them the *same* expressions are to be interpreted in the *same* way, but this does not indicate *what justifies the assumption*. All understanding of the speech of another involves radical interpretation. (Davidson, 1984d: 125, italics added)

At the core of interpreting a speaker's linguistic expressions are mechanisms and challenges that are very similar to those related to understanding foreign expressions. Therefore, when Davidson examines instances of interpreting one language into another – where the need for interpretation may be more apparent – it is only to elucidate what is assumed in comprehending the meaning of expressions conveyed in any language.

The analytic philosophy of language proposed by Quine and Davidson entered the debate in Translation Studies especially because of their focus on the variety of conceptual schemes linked to different languages, questioning the notion of meaning itself and possibly leading to relativistic outcomes in translation (Malmkjær, 2005: ch. 3). However, some scholars have argued that 'with the honourable exceptions of the Americans W. V. O. Quine and Donald Davidson . . .even the linguistically orientated analytical philosophy of the postwar period has generally failed to engage with the topic' (Large, 2014: 182–3; see also Pym, 2007; Arrojo, 2010).

The first objective of the Element is to show that Quine and Davidson did not abruptly make central the issue of translation that had been ignored by their colleagues, but rather gave it greater and strategically different importance in analytic philosophy. To this aim, the Element historically reconstructs the main phases of the reflection on translation in analytic philosophy, presenting the different views on translation provided by giants in analytic philosophy who are often neglected in Translation Studies, but might be of extreme interest, especially for translation theory. In this perspective, Quine's mental experiment on radical translation would not unexpectedly enter the scene of analytic philosophy, as Carnap and Wittgenstein already presented it, within different theoretical frameworks which offer fundamental tools to study translation and translation-related conceptual issues.

The second objective of the Element is to highlight the shortcomings of analytic philosophy when investigating the problem of translation. The main limitations of analytic philosophy in the study of translation, which also prevent Translation Studies scholars from approaching it, can be identified with the use of specific formal methods that are applied to formalized languages rather than natural languages, and with the language-centric and artificial use of translation examples which often lacks representation of actual translation practice. In particular, the Anglophone nature of the analytic tradition, especially in the post-war period, deeply influenced not only research on the linguistic aspects of translation but also the cultural approach to translation.

Thus, the method of analytic philosophy itself is a double-edged sword for the study of translation: on the one hand, it can provide useful insights for the conceptual clarification of different theoretical problems involved in translation, but on the other hand, it can propose an idealized version of translation bringing scholars far away from the real linguistic and cultural challenges of translation. This Element aims to bring to light the main contributions to translation theory coming from analytic philosophy, and the ways to highlight the limitations mentioned earlier in contemporary analytic philosophy.

Therefore, the sections composing the Element examine the different view of translation provided by the main philosophers in the history of analytic philosophy, from the beginnings to nowadays. Section 1 considers the definition of translation as paraphrase, referring to some works by Gottlob Frege, Bertrand Russell, and Rudolf Carnap, the 'father founders' of analytic philosophy of language and of the method itself of analysis as translation of natural language into a clearer 'logical' language. Section 2 is dedicated to two views of translation proposed by Ludwig Wittgenstein: translation as calculus in the *Tractatus logico-philosophicus* (1921, hereafter 'TLP') and translation as a language game in *Philosophical Investigations* (1953, hereafter 'PI'). In this latter work, Wittgenstein harshly criticized his own previous view of translation, taking distance from Carnap's view of translation and, in general, from the assumptions on language shared by the Vienna Circle, to which Carnap belonged.

The problem of conceptual relativism and the very idea of a conceptual scheme, as suggested by Hans-Johann Glock in the analysis of the Wittgensteinian texts, will be the point of contact with the following sections on Quine and Davidson. In Section 3, the famous Quinean mental experiment of radical translation will be presented, showing that the radical difference among conceptual schemes associated with languages brings Quine to dramatic consequences for translation. Section 4 shows that his radical holism and relativism directly stem from the dissolution of the notion of meaning he operated in *Two Dogmas of Empiricism* (Quine, 1953). However, Section 5 aims to show that Davidson rightly criticized the third dogma of Empiricism, that is, the distinction between conceptual scheme and empirical content, offering a powerful argument to overcome Quine's conceptual relativism and consequent outcomes for translation.

Section 6 will focus on the concept of semantic equivalence in Davidson's *A Nice Derangement of Epitaphs* (1986), comparing it with Wilfrid Sellars' notion of pragmatic equivalence, which proves to be too vague but still necessary to grasp some aspects of meaning going beyond the semantic realm. Section 7 is further dedicated to the 'pragmatic side' of meaning in translation, which was put aside by the philosophers of ideal language, such as Frege, but finally acquired a prominent position in ordinary language philosophy. More specifically, the section is devoted to the problem of translating the implicit meaning of a text into another language in the Gricean framework, which provides valuable insights for both translation theory and practice. Indeed, within the analytic tradition, ordinary language philosophy differs from ideal language philosophy, precisely in the method which looks at real human interactions in conversational contexts rather than regimented language.

Following Paul Grice, Saul Kripke (1979) distinguished between what words mean and what the speaker meant by using those words in a given context, and used translation as a test to identify meaning ambiguity in the original text. Alberto Voltolini (2009) proposed to strengthen Kripke's test, arguing that any linguistic phenomenon in the original text is genuinely semantic if it can be solved through translation, forcing the translator to choose between two different senses in the words of another language. A linguistic phenomenon would be genuinely pragmatic if it can be preserved in translation. Section 8, I will introduce Kripke's test and its strengthened version and will argue that translation does not work as a test to distinguish between semantic and pragmatic phenomena, but it can instead work as a test for the distinction between explicit and implicit phenomena of meaning.

In Section 9, in light of the contemporary debate between Literalism and Contextualism, I will claim that the difference between the original and the alternative translations is the result of a change in the degree of explicitness in translation. What is crucial to translation is that languages differ in the strategies used to make meaning explicit, in both their pragmatic processes of enrichment and impoverishment (Carston, 2002). These processes draw information, not only from the original sentence but also from the context.

In the conclusion section, the Element provides other sources for discussion and future directions, to show how contemporary analytic philosophers are facing the main limitations of the methodological approach to translation. This includes new formal methods, such as logical pluralism, and new disruptive research themes, such as the problem of linguistic injustice in a language-centric philosophical tradition. While attracting increasing interest and potentially providing new venues for research on translation from an analytic-philosophical perspective, they question the very nature of analytic philosophy and its traditional method, as well as its ability to still provide a significant contribution to clarifying the problem of translation.

1 From Frege to Carnap: Translation as Paraphrase

Translation has been a central problem in analytic philosophy of language from the very beginning: the very idea of 'analysis' in analytic philosophy of language requires the concept of translation. Indeed, as pointed out, the concept of analysis itself as a philosophical method rests on translation, and especially on the 'translational' notion of analysis as a paraphrase: 'here, the original idea was to rephrase ordinary sentences that appeared to raise philosophical difficulties in such a way that difficulties would disappear' (Marconi, 2019: 349). Arising at the beginning of the century as a technical problem within a specific objective (reducing mathematics to logic, that is, one formal language to another), the problem of translation changed in the 1930s to that of finding a general method for translating formalized languages, and by the end of the 1950s it became one of delineating the general conditions of translation, independent of the type of languages involved (Morra, 2009).

The essay *Über Sinn und Bedeutung* (*On Sense and Reference*, 1892) by Frege is believed to be the origin of the analytic school of thought, and it discusses translation. In the essay, Frege explores the conditions necessary for an exact translation, including the possibility of constructing mathematics solely from logical concepts and statements through a mechanical method or calculation. Frege acknowledges that fully translating the meaning of an expression into another language is partially indeterminate, as only the *reference* (what it denotes) and *sense* (the conceptualization of the reference from a particular point of view – for example, '7' and '5 + 2' both denote the same number but in different ways) are objective and identical across languages.

In particular, the sense is part of the 'common treasure of thoughts', which is 'transmitted from generation to generation' (Frege, 1892: 29). Only the reference and sense of expressions are objective and therefore shareable, and, above all, contribute to the truth value of the statements of which the expressions are part. Frege thus believes that a translation must preserve these two components of meaning: reference and sense. On the contrary, differences in communicative content or effect should not be considered as differences in meaning, but rather as differences in *tone*. Such differences only serve to 'colour' the communicative content of an expression and are thus excluded from a sentence's meaning.

> The difference between a translation and the original text should properly not overstep the first level [the level of ideas]. To the possible differences here belong also the colouring and shading which poetic eloquence seeks to give to the sense. Such colouring and shading are not objective, and must be evoked by each hearer or reader according to the hints of the poet or the speaker. Without some affinity in human ideas art would certainly be impossible; but it can never be exactly determined how far the intentions of the poet are realized. (Frege, 1892: 27)

Because tone is subjective, it cannot be considered part of a rigorous, precise science. In other words, while a translation may vary in appropriateness and overall communicative content based on context, a good translation should maintain meaning, but need not preserve the tone or communicative effect, also known as the 'pragmatic side' of meaning. Thus, the limitation of the Fregean definition of translation is that it does not consider the pragmatic aspects of meaning. Other analytic philosophers, such as Sellars (see Section 6), and especially philosophers of ordinary language, such as Grice (see Section 7), will later propose theoretical frameworks focusing on the 'pragmatic side' of meaning in translation.

In Frege's view, in that particular type of translation which is the logical reduction of mathematical statements, the pragmatic aspect of meaning, is not at play. There is a method to verify if this is the case: for a statement, the translation preserves the truth value when substituting all its parts with expressions of the same truth conditions, and the sense when it can be replaced in the compositional sentences of which it is a component without modifying its truth value. For instance, when replacing 'dead' with the term 'deceased', having a different tone but the same truth conditions, the truth value of the sentence 'Berlusconi is dead' remains unaltered. Indeed, Frege believed that the calculation necessary to reconstruct mathematics starting from logic could have a determined outcome, because – to transmit the content of logic statements unaltered – it is sufficient to preserve the reference and sense of the expressions that form them, the only components of the meaning that affect the truth value of sentences, and whose translation is precisely determined.

Instead, the mental images and associations that are connected to a specific expression cannot be guaranteed to be the same in another language: differently from the term 'dead', the term 'deceased' can only be associated with a person and may evoke a more detached attitude toward that person. These representations not only differ between individuals but also rely on the unique 'psychological husk' of the language in which the expression is used. This husk is responsible for shaping the grammar of thoughts and plays a role in determining belief attribution in translation (Santambrogio, 2002). As Frege wrote (1879–1891: 6):

> Grammar ... is a mixture of the logical and the psychological. Otherwise all languages would necessarily have the same grammar. Can the same thought be expressed in different languages? Without a doubt, so far as the logical kernel is concerned; for otherwise it would not be possible for human beings to share a common intellectual life. But if we think of the kernel with the psychological husk added, a precise translation is impossible. ... From this we can see the value of learning languages for one's logical education; when we see that the same thought can be worded in different ways, our mind separates off the husk from the kernel, though, in any given language, it appears as a natural and integral part of it. This is how the differences between languages can facilitate our grasp of what is logical.

As pointed out (Marconi, 2019), Frege intended his formal language to serve as a substitute for natural language in scientific contexts, rather than as a means of paraphrasing the 'true' meanings. Nevertheless, since formulas could be clarified by translating them into natural sentences, they were frequently seen as conveying the same concepts that were expressed, frequently more ambiguously, by natural language. Also, Russell's analysis should be seen on the background of Frege's creation of a formal language: his work on definite descriptions in *On Denoting* (Russell, 1905) shows that problematic sentences concerning non-existent objects, such as 'The present king of France is bald', can be *paraphrased* into the following sentences that make it clear that it is false and not about non-existent objects: (a) there exists something that is the present king of France; (b) there is only one thing that is the present king of France; and (c) anything that is the present king of France is bald. Russell is thus 'better associated with the notion of analysis as *paraphrase*, of which his treatment of definite descriptions would become a paradigm' (Marconi, 2019: 348, italics added).

Russell was an influential figure among the analytic philosophers who came later: they viewed analysis as a *process of rephrasing* problematic sentences into clearer and unambiguous sentences, while retaining their meaning. This activity was explicitly performed by analytic philosophers to uncover the 'true meaning' of a sentence, which they believed to be hidden by its surface-level grammatical structure. For instance, Carnap employed paraphrases in his *Logische Syntax der Sprache* (*Logical Syntax of Language*, 1934) to demonstrate that sentences regarding objects were, in fact, referring to words by translating them into the 'formal mode of speech'.[2] Carnap indeed shared his philosophical framework with the Vienna Circle, a group of philosophers and scientists in the early twentieth century, who sought to establish a unified approach to knowledge based on logical positivism. Thus, Carnap, a prominent member of the Vienna Circle, contributed to the development of logical syntax, but also to the verification principle, according to which an expression is only meaningful if it can be verified through empirical observation or logical proof, as key tenets of their philosophical programme.

Overturning the explanatory priority from reference to meaning, Carnap emphasized the importance of formal relationships between expressions within a language when it comes to translation. His conventionalist stance created the basis for comparing propositions across languages, not based on reality but on a third language that connects the source and target languages. As Carnap explained (1934: § 32), this operation has the form of a *calculus*:

> The interpretation of a language is a translation and therefore something which can be *formally represented*; the reconstruction and examination of interpretations belong to formal syntax. This holds equally of an interpretation of, say, French in German when what is required is not merely some kind of transformance in respect of sentences, but, as we say, a rendering of the sense or meaning of the French sentences. . . . In the case of an individual language like German, the construction of the syntax of that language means the construction of a calculus that fulfils the condition of being in agreement with the actual historical habits of speech in German-speaking people. And the construction of the calculus must take place entirely within the domain of formal syntax, although the decision as to whether the calculus fulfils the given condition is not a logical but a historical and empirical one, which lies outside the domain of pure syntax. The same thing holds, analogously, for the relation between two languages designated as translation or interpretation.

Carnap defines the meaning of a sentence as the set of sentences that follow from it (i.e., having a consequence relation), and he presents a method to explicitly identify the formal implications that stem from adopting a system of symbol connection in translation. If the relations of consequence that determine if a sentence belongs to the set of consequences of another sentence can be

---

[2] As remarked (Marconi, 2019: 354): 'It should be added that the model of analysis as paraphrase had not been entirely obliterated in the 1930s and 1940s, even aside from Carnap's essential contribution', but the most important innovation came later with Richard M. Montague's 'rigorization of paraphrase' in formal semantics (Montague, 1973).

defined in both languages involved in a translation, and if a language is provided to formulate the syntax of both languages and establish a one-to-many correspondence between their types of elements (symbols, expressions, sentences) while preserving the logical consequence relationship between sentences, it is possible to contrast the sets of sentences that are consequences of those related through translation. Actually, Carnap proposes a *scalar notion of translation*, which considers a syntactic correlation one-to-many (Morra, 2009).

For a translation to be reversible, there must be a unique correlation between the elements of one expressive level in the languages being translated. However, if the correlation between simple symbols is not one-to-one, then the translation is only reversible for the corresponding transposed expressive elements. This is because even if a symbol in the target language does not have a direct counterpart in the source language, its components can be combined to form an equivalent symbol. The preservation of meaning is only completely achieved through an isomorphic translation. When dealing with compound expressions or sentences, a bijective correspondence (i.e., a correspondence creating a connection between two sets where each symbol from one set is matched with a symbol from the other set) can only preserve the truth conditions and truth value of the text. Despite the possibility of correlating multiple equivalent meanings to higher-level syntactic objects, a choice must be made based on extra-syntactic factors. Carnap argues that this choice can be formalized, ensuring that translation remains an operation with a determined outcome (Ervas & Morra, 2013).

When Carnap moved to the United States in 1935, he placed more importance on the correlation between signs and their designated meanings. He was persuaded by Tarski's formalization of the truth concept (Tarski, 1933), which led him to believe that the syntactic method could be integrated with a semantics system, to be expressed in a richer language to establish the truth conditions for each sentence. In *Meaning and Necessity: A Study in Semantics and Modal Logic* (1947), Carnap proposed that if two different languages express the same individual concept, property, or proposition, and if their semantic rules establish that they refer to the same individual, group of individuals, or truth value, then they have the same intension,[3] that is, L-equivalence. However, the L-equivalence of sentences may not be sufficient for an exact translation:

> If we ask for an exact translation of a given statement, say the exact translation of a scientific hypothesis or of the testimony of a witness in court from

---

[3] The *intension* of an expression refers to its meaning (or conceptual content), whereas its *extension* includes everything that represents or exemplifies the meaning (or conceptual content). For instance, the intension of 'ship' as a noun is 'vehicle for transporting something on water', whereas its extension embraces such things as cargo ships, passenger ships, battleships, and sailing ships.

French into English, we should usually require much more than agreement in the intensions of the sentences, that is L-equivalence of the sentences. Even if we restrict our attention to designative (cognitive) meaning – leaving aside other meaning components like the emotive and the motivative, although they are often very important even for the translation of theoretical texts – L-equivalence of sentences is not sufficient; it will be required that at least some of the component designator be L-equivalent, in other words, that the intensional structures be alike or at least similar. (Carnap, 1947: 59–60)

His refinement of the concepts of meaning and synonymy led to a more nuanced understanding of translation fidelity. A translation can be equivalent in meaning (having the same truth value), logically equivalent (having the same truth conditions), isomorphic (having equivalent symbols), or intensionally iso-morphic (having elements with the same intension as their counterparts in the sentence). The last case recreates an analogous relational structure and fully preserves meaning (Ervas & Morra, 2013).

Carnap maintained an interest in natural languages and viewed them as systems of habits that produce specific sounds for various actions such as communication or influencing thoughts. In line with the main assumption of the analytic philosophy of ideal language, he believed that a theory of transla-tion, which eliminates expressive ambiguities, could be applied to natural languages just as it is applied to formalized languages. Thus, Carnap shared with his predecessors in analytic philosophy of ideal language, Frege and Russell, the idea that translation works in natural languages in the same way as in formalized languages, once the 'pragmatic side' of natural languages has been eliminated. This is of course a limitation for the study of translation in natural languages, which are contextual- and cultural-dependent, a limitation that analytic philosophers of ordinary language aimed to overcome (see Section 7).

Carnap held the belief that the extension and intension of formal constructs could also be identified within natural languages. Carnap acknowledged that when dealing with an unfamiliar verbal system, the cognitive-explanatory process from intension to extension is reversed. Observers must analyse the linguistic reactions of speakers to events and their non-linguistic behaviour in the world to understand the system, as intensions are inherently linked to an unknown linguistic context. Therefore, to establish possible equivalence rules with symbols from one's language to another, one must first determine the extension of certain expressions in the unknown language, and then analyse their intensions. Although an extension may have multiple corresponding intensions, observing the behaviour of speakers can narrow down the potential range of the extension. In *Introduction to Semantics* (1942), he wrote:

Descriptive semantics and syntax [as opposed to pure semantics and syntax] are indeed based on pragmatics. Suppose we wish to study the semantical and syntactical properties of a certain Eskimo language not previously investigated. Obviously, there is no other way than first to observe the speaking habits of the people who use it. Only after finding by observation the pragmatical fact that those people have the habit of using the word 'igloo' when they intended to refer to a house are we in a position to make the semantical statement '"igloo" means (designates) house' and the syntactical statement '"igloo" is a predicate'. (Carnap, 1942: 12–13)

Later, Carnap described an imaginary scenario in which a linguist with no knowledge of the German language attempted to learn it by observing the linguistic behaviour of native speakers. The linguist reduced the discussion to the meaning of a few predicates, and from there attempted to determine their extension. To achieve this, the linguist would need to verify, via verbal expressions of a German speaker, which things those predicates would denote according to that individual speaker.

The relationship between the intension and the extension of an expression was also at the centre of Quine's philosophical interests. Quine instead argued that it was impossible to determine a specific intension to be linked with the expression of an unknown language based on the linguistic behaviour of its speakers (Quine, 1953, see also Section 3). In *Meaning and Synonymy in Natural Languages* (1955), Carnap explicitly denied that the aim of his work is to defend

the thesis that the analysis of intension for a natural language is a scientific procedure, methodologically just as sound as the analysis of extension. . . . The core of the controversy [with Quine] concerns the nature of a linguist's assignment of one of these properties to the predicate as its intension. . . . The *intensionalist thesis* in pragmatics, which I am defending, says that the assignment of an intension is an empirical hypothesis which, like any other hypothesis in linguistics, can be tested by observations of language behavior. On the other hand, the *extensionalist thesis* asserts that the assignment of an intension, on the basis of the previously determined extension, is not a question of fact but merely a matter of choice. The thesis holds that the linguist is free to choose any of those properties which fit to the given extension; he may be guided in his choice by a consideration of simplicity, but there is no question of right or wrong. (Carnap, 1955: 236–7)

Carnap concluded that this approach would lead to many doubts and mistakes, as both the German speaker and the linguist could make errors. Moreover, 'the generalization to things which he [the linguist] has not tested suffers, of course, from the uncertainty of all inductive inference' (Carnap, 1955: 236). Thus, Carnap anticipated the possible outcomes of the Quinean extentionalist thesis (see Section 3), while moving toward a more pragmatic direction with his intensionalist thesis.

2 Wittgenstein: Translation as Calculus and Translation as a Language Game

The reflection on translation also had an impact on Wittgenstein's work (Oliveira et al., 2019). As is well known, his early works presuppose logical atomism for translatability, while his later works focus on grammar and language games. Consequently, the author consistently addresses the question of what conditions enable translation in his philosophical approach. The fact that the term *Übersetzung* ('translation') and related words appear 505 times in Wittgenstein's collected works is a clear demonstration of the ongoing interest in the translation issue. This is a significant number of occurrences, as it is almost as frequent as the term *Sprachspiel* ('language game'), which is extensively studied and debated among scholars (Montibeller, 2009).

In the *Logisch-philosophische Abhandlung* (*Tractatus logico-philosophicus*, 1921, TLP), Wittgenstein described translation as a formal and necessary relationship between propositions in different languages, based on the reference of words, which is the first component of meaning identified by Frege. Wittgenstein posited that different languages are concrete manifestations of the same primary language of thought, and that their propositions, depicting the same state of affairs, are intertranslatable: 'If I know the meaning of an English and a synonymous German word, it is impossible for me not to know that they are synonymous, it is impossible for me not to be able to translate them into one another' (TLP, 4.243). In particular, the elementary object is seen as a crucial requirement for translation and the ultimate point of reference for verifying whether two statements are describing the same thing (see TLP, 4.21–4.431, 5.3–5.41). However, the object can only be understood in a propositional context where it is defined through its relationships with other objects to create a state of affairs. Though an object is defined as remaining stable despite changes in relationships, its definition is dependent upon comprehending the relationships in which it exists, and this is an essential prerequisite for translatability (Ervas & Morra, 2013).

According to his perspective, when translating a sentence to a different language, it is necessary to deconstruct it using the logical syntax rules that are consistent across multiple languages. This involved identifying the names of the objects represented in the source language and finding equivalent names in the target language. By applying the same syntactic rules to the equivalent names, a proposition similar to the original sentence could be automatically created. In Wittgenstein's words (TLP, 3.343): 'Definitions are rules for the translation of one language into another. Every correct symbolism must be translatable into every other according to such rules. It is this which all have in common.' In this perspective, translation is a *calculus* that does not require any interpretive effort, and like any calculation, it is a completely reversible operation: the set of rules that determined a translation, applied in reverse, reproduces exactly the original source text. As Wittgenstein remarked in the *Tractatus* (TLP, 4.0141), using the metaphor of the gramophone record:

> In the fact that there is a general rule by which the musician is able to read the symphony out of the score, and that there is a rule by which one could reconstruct the symphony from the line on a gramophone record and from this again – by means of the first rule – construct the score, herein lies the international similarity between these things which at first sight seem to be entirely different. And the rule is the law of projection which projects the symphony into the language of the gramophone record.

While Carnap concluded that there was a need to create a translation calculus that was not based on a triangulation from one language to reality and then to another language (see Section 1), Wittgenstein's theory only ensured the consistency of meaning in translation if languages are isomorphic to the world. In the *Tractatus* (1921), an elementary proposition is considered true only if the state of affairs it describes is actually occurring, thus 'the translation of one language into another is not a process of translating each proposition of the one into a proposition of the other, but only the constituent parts of propositions are translated' (TLP, 4.025). However, this is a metaphysical assumption that contradicts the neopositivist scientific ideal. Thus, Wittgenstein later rejected the *picture theory of meaning* and the accompanying metaphysical concept of states of affairs. Rejecting this hypothesis challenges the assurance of reversible transformation of scientific laws. The meaning of these laws is defined by the overall conceptualization of observation statements, rather than just the individual sensory primitives they rely on for their basis.

Between 1930 and 1933, Wittgenstein also rethought the correlation between language and the world. He viewed translation as a *calculation that occurs against the backdrop of a third language*, and like Carnap, he believed that translating involves selecting one of the potential correlations between different symbols of languages (see Section 1). This choice is based on the aspects used to equate the symbols calibrated for the purpose of the translation. Unlike Carnap, Wittgenstein believed that interpretation is involved from the beginning of the process, not just at the end. Thus, the semantic level of the translation process does not follow the syntactic level, but rather precedes it. Indeed, while for

Carnap interpretation is an additional translation following the translation process itself, closed in relation to it, for Wittgenstein it is an integral part of the process, determining every single step (Montibeller, 2009; Morra, 2009). This is because at each stage it is necessary to decide whether the current general translation rule is still appropriate or should be changed. This decision is made by comparing the current rule with other possible rules, which are constructed in opposition to it at the moment. If one supposes that selecting a certain translation rule over others can be justified and has clear results, then translating becomes a fully precise calculation with no room for uncertainty.

This view of translation has the merit of seeing translation as a process rather than a product. However, Wittgenstein himself acknowledged the shortcomings of this view. Indeed, during his study of everyday language forms, Wittgenstein discovered that not all the reasons for choosing a particular translation between natural languages can be formalized. This means that attaining complete accuracy in translation calculation is impossible in these languages (Ervas & Morra, 2013). In natural languages, a translation alters the message conveyed in an irreversible manner as it substitutes the original expressions with different structured phrases. Nonetheless, this does not necessarily diminish its efficiency. Translation models, such as the one proposed by the *Tractatus*, are only applicable to languages whose names refer to a single set of simple objects identified by thought, which is an unlikely hypothesis when applied to natural languages. If the translation, given the formal strategy discussed in the *Tractatus*, could take place almost mechanically, now the problem arises of interpreting the meaning of the words that must be used so that any rule can apply to the wider linguistic context that the author targets. To accommodate the broader research context, a more universal theory of translation was necessary, one that is not restricted by the specific features of the languages involved, but rather designed to address the complexities of natural languages (see Wilson, 2016).

The ideas of the *Tractatus* inspired the Vienna Circle philosophers to develop the project of logical analysis further. They sought to eliminate metaphysical and meaningless claims from philosophy, and instead promote a scientific and logical approach to understanding the world. They saw themselves as continuing and expanding upon Wittgenstein's work, refining and systematizing his ideas. While he provided them with a framework for analysing language, emphasizing logical relationships, and promoting empiricism, Wittgenstein himself never became a member of the Vienna Circle, distancing himself from its members and harshly criticizing them, Carnap included.

Wittgenstein criticized the Vienna Circle primarily due to their adherence to logical positivism and their excessive reliance on the verification principle (see Section 1), which was rightly perceived as overly restrictive and led to the exclusion of important aspects of language and meaning. Wittgenstein advocated for a broader understanding of language and meaning that incorporates the complexities and nuances of human communication. Wittgenstein also rightly accused the Vienna Circle of attempting to solve philosophical problems by reducing them to scientific or logical issues. Indeed, many philosophical problems cannot be resolved through empirical or scientific methods alone, as they involve deep-seated conceptual confusions or misunderstandings.

The cultural environment in Vienna had an important influence on the development of Wittgenstein's thought (Janik & Toulmin, 1973), but in Cambridge, discussing his ideas with his students, other analytic philosophers, and great economists, such as John Maynard Keynes and Piero Sraffa, Wittgenstein changed his mind on the nature of language. Wittgenstein now claimed that not all meaningful statements can be reduced to empirical observations, as language serves various purposes beyond simple empirical description. He emphasized the importance of *language games* (PI, 7, 24) and the contextual nature of language, asserting that meaning is derived from its *use* in specific social, cultural, and linguistic contexts. This was a revolution within the analytic philosophy of language, which in some way placed the 'second' or later Wittgenstein outside of analytical philosophy itself, in terms of content and method.

In this new perspective, there is no systematic way to translate into every language. Translation does not result in a predetermined outcome either before or after the translation process. This is due to the fact that translation is not a mechanical calculation that is necessarily linked to reality, and the rules governing translation have a structurally contingent nature. Furthermore, these rules are not only created for the specific translation task but they do not even obtain necessary characteristics during the process. Translation is like a mathematical problem that, like the translation of a poem or a joke, has no systematic method for solution:

> Translating from one language into another is a mathematical task, and the translation of a lyrical poem, for example, into a foreign language is quite analogous to a mathematical problem. For one may well frame the problem 'How is this joke (e.g.) to be translated (i.e., replaced) by a joke in the other language?' and this problem can be solved; but there was no systematic method of solving it. (Wittgenstein, 1929–1948: 698)

In the first section of the *Philosophische Untersuchungen* (*Philosophical Investigations*, 1953, PI), translation is viewed as a language game with a range of rules that are adaptable during play. The application of these rules is unpredictable, both in relation to the meaning of expressions, which are strictly tied to the linguistic usage context, and their reference, which are not assignable to any particular observation as it is the whole language that is put forward to reality, not just the propositions or ostensive definitions upon which it is based. It may become clear why the term *Übersetzungsregel* ('translation rule') ceases to appear in Wittgenstein's manuscripts (Montibeller, 2009). When moving from the realm of natural sciences to that of everyday language renders the notion of discovering a universally applicable set of guidelines for interpretation, like the one he initially proposed, implausible. Instead, one can only comprehend a *grammar* (PI, 90) and subsequently adapt it to another language by articulating it as a translation.

Now, the concept of grammar becomes central because language games are no longer conceived as a set of symbols, as in formalized languages of natural sciences, but rather as an *activity* based on a form of life (PI, 19, 23). Against the views of his predecessors on language, the 'second' Wittgenstein presented multiple examples, such as translation, to clarify the diversity and complexity of language games:

> Consider the variety of language games in the following examples, and in others:
>
> Giving orders, and acting on them –
> Describing an object by its the appearance, or by its measurements –
> Constructing an object from a description (a drawing) –
> Reporting an event –
> Speculating about the event –
> Forming and testing a hypothesis –
> Presenting the results of an experiment in tables and diagrams –
> Making up a story; and reading one –
> Acting in a play –
> Singing rounds –
> Guessing riddles –
> Cracking a joke; telling one –
> Solving a problem in practical arithmetic –
> *Translating from one language into another* –
> Asking, thanking, cursing, greeting, praying.
> – It is interesting to compare the diversity of the tools of language and of the ways they are used, the diversity of kinds of word and sentence, with what logicians have said about the structure of language. (This includes the author of the *Tractatus Logico-Philosophicus*.) (PI, 23, italics added)

Taking distance from his own previous philosophical ideas, Wittgenstein now sees language as not separate from thought, because thought itself is also rooted in our language as a form of life (PI, 241). Therefore, a language cannot precede thought and is instead an integral part of the same form of life, we simply 'translate' thought into language:

> What happens when we make an effort – say in writing a letter – to find the right expression for our thoughts? – This way of speaking compares the process to one of translating or describing: the thoughts are already there (perhaps were there in advance) and we merely look for their expression. This picture is more or less appropriate in different cases. (PI, 335)

Thus, the issue is not simply aligning words with an ambiguous 'reality', but rather understanding how one's personal interpretive system operates and can be translated into language. Additionally, in the case of translation, Wittgenstein suggests the presence of a primal and profound mode of thought that engages in a dialectic with the more articulate thoughts that can be expressed through words in different languages:

> Just as Germanisms creep into the speech of a German who speaks English well although he does not first construct the German expression and then translate it into English; just as this makes him speak English as if he were translating 'unconsciously' from the German – so we often think as if our thinking were founded on a thought-schema: as if we were translating from a more primitive mode of thought into ours. (PI, 38)

In the *Philosophical Investigations* (PI, 32), Wittgenstein imagined the situation of a foreigner who wants to learn another language in the following way: 'Someone coming into a foreign country will sometimes learn the language of the inhabitants from ostensive explanations that they give him; and he will often have to *guess* how to interpret these explanations; and sometimes he will guess right, sometimes wrong.' Later, in *Meaning and Synonymy in Natural Languages* (1955), Carnap would propose a similar imagined scenario to determine a predicate extension via translation (see Section 2). Through the experiment of radical translation, Quine takes up and develops the translation problem brought up by Wittgenstein and Carnap in a relativistic and 'radical' way.

However, as Hans-Johann Glock (2007: 380) argued, though Wittgenstein, in his later works, is commonly considered as a representative of relativism, his 'account of truth never set him on a slippery slope to ontological relativism'. In Glock's interpretation, while Quine did adhere to ontological relativism (see Section 3), Wittgenstein was more aligned with conceptual relativism. Davidson will attack conceptual relativism and the dogma of the existence of radically different conceptual schemes that organize empirical content differently (see Section 4). A conceptual scheme can be compared to what Wittgenstein refers to as a *grammar*. The grammar of a language consists of the rules that define it, including not only grammatical rules but also those that dictate what is meaningful to say.

3 Quine and the Thesis of Translation Indeterminacy

In the book *Word and Object* (1960) and later in the article *Ontological Relativity* (1968), Quine proposed that a linguist only knows their own language (L') and should attempt to translate the native speaker's language (L) by observing their *dispositions towards verbal behaviour*. Quine's groundbreaking experiment in radical translation aims to uncover the mechanisms and challenges of understanding a foreign language by making the conditions for translation more extreme. In a situation of radical translation, the linguist cannot rely on a translation manual that renders the unknown language into a known language. The linguist also lacks any knowledge of the customs or beliefs of the linguistic community speaking the foreign language. Through observing the behavioural dispositions, however, the linguist can establish 'some equations' between sentences in the source language (L) and the target language (L'). As Quine wrote to Reuben Brower: 'I imagine that a good deal of translating depends on observing equations between native sentences, without any clear notion of what one or other of the sentences stands for' (Morra, 2004: 257).

To accomplish this in the context of radical translation, a linguist must create a translation manual (T), which is a set of rules that enables the translation of any utterance (A) from language L to language L'. To be deemed correct, (T) must adhere to a strict set of behavioural constraints. The correct conditions of (T) are solely based on the speaker's behavioural tendencies: a manual will be considered correct if the situations in which an L-speaker is inclined to use (A) correspond to those in which L'-speakers are inclined to use T(A), that is, the set of expressions of L' that (T) associates with (A).

In the experiment of radical translation, both the linguist and the native speaker observe a rabbit. The native speaker utters 'gavagai' upon seeing the rabbit, and the linguist notes that this happens whenever a rabbit is present. Based on observing a strong correlation between the presence of a rabbit and the utterance of 'gavagai' by the native speaker, the linguist infers that 'gavagai' means 'rabbit'. However, this initial analytical hypothesis must be confirmed by the linguist by questioning the native speaker to confirm that the translation of 'gavagai' actually is 'rabbit'.

The meaning of a sentence, as a stimulus to verbal behaviour, is determined by the type of response it elicits from the native speaker. If a sentence prompts agreement in the native speaker, it has an affirmative stimulus meaning. Conversely, if it prompts disagreement, it has a negative stimulus meaning. To test this hypothesis, the linguist must first determine the signs of agreement or disagreement by observing the native's reactions to questions. The linguist should guess from observation and then see how well his guesses work. Thus suppose that in asking 'Gavagai?' and the like, in the conspicuous presence of rabbits and the like, he has elicited the responses 'Evet' and 'Yok' often enough to surmise that they may correspond to 'Yes' and 'No', but has no notion which is which. Then he tries the experiment of echoing the native's own volunteered pronouncements. If thereby he pretty regularly elicits 'Evet' rather than 'Yok', he is encouraged to take 'Evet' as 'Yes'. Also he tries responding with 'Evet' and 'Yok' to the native's remarks; the one that is the more serene in its effect is the better candidate for 'Yes'. However inconclusive these methods, they generate a working hypothesis. If extraordinary difficulties attend all his subsequent steps, the linguist may decide to discard that hypothesis and guess again. (Quine, 1960: 26)

In radical translation, a dialogue occurs that brings the linguist closer and closer to the '*stimulus meaning*' of the sentence 'gavagai'. Quine defines the stimulus meaning of a sentence as an ordered pair (*affirmative stimulus meaning, negative stimulus meaning*): the affirmative stimulus meaning is the class of all stimuli that would prompt the speaker to assent to the sentence, while the negative stimulus meaning is the class of all stimuli that would lead the speaker to dissent.

This type of research enables the translation of *observation sentences*. These sentences have the same stimulus meaning for every speaker of the foreign language because everyone is predisposed to agree in similar circumstances. Observation sentences are part of a broader group called *occasion sentences*, which differ from *standing sentences*. In occasion sentences, agreement or disagreement is based on the stimulation of the moment, without referencing learned knowledge or beliefs. In contrast, in standing sentences, agreement or disagreement is given without this type of stimulation: standing sentences are indeed those that are assumed to be true and serve as a foundation for further inquiry and knowledge, such as basic empirical statements or logical truths.

The linguist should begin by translating observation sentences to recognize the use of truth-functional connectives in the foreign grammar structure. Through this process, the linguist can even determine when two different sentences have the same stimulus meaning (are *stimulus synonymous*), when the speakers always agree with the sentence (which is then *stimulus analytic*), and when the speakers always disagree with the sentence (which then displays *stimulus contradictoriness*).[4] Once the linguist has gathered this information,

---

[4] For example, according to Quine, a case of stimulus synonymy could be of two words/phrases, 'bachelor' and 'unmarried man', which have the same stimulus meaning. A case of stimulus analyticity could be '2 + 2 = 4' or 'No bachelor is married', to which speakers always give their assent. The opposite case is that of stimulus contradictoriness: speakers always give their dissent to the 'stimulus-contradictory' sentences (See Quine, 1960: 46–57).

they can use the native's answers and the level of their command of the target language to formulate a system of *analytical hypotheses*. This system will serve as the overall hypothesis of the grammatical-syntactical structures and stimulus meanings, which will guide the linguist in creating the translation manual.

If the sensory stimulation that leads both the linguist and the speaker to agree (or disagree) on an observation sentence is the same, then the linguist will attribute the same meaning to the recurring term in the sentence that the native speaker had attributed to that term. However, this operation implies that the term refers to the same object and not others. It is assumed that there is an *identity of extension* of the term for both the linguist and the native speaker, and the term has the same reference for both. Quine argues that if the linguist assigns the term 'gagavai' to rabbits, it does not mean that the native cannot use that term to refer to a 'rabbit-stage' or a 'rabbit-phase'. In this case, 'gagavai' could refer to, for instance, an 'undetached rabbit part'! Quine's *thesis of the inscrutability of reference* claims that equally correct translation manuals might translate the same words using completely different references.

Thus, nothing makes the translation of 'gagavai' to 'rabbit' more appropriate than 'part of an undetached rabbit'. The linguist may find the translation of 'gagavai' to 'rabbit' more likely than 'temporal stage of a rabbit' or 'part of an undetached rabbit'. However, this is because the linguist assumes that the foreign speaker's *conceptual scheme* is equivalent to their own and that a specific reference notion linked to the extensional conception of meaning is valid. Quine argues that this assumption cannot be proven. Imposing a translation means attributing a particular segmentation to the native language and a way of perceiving the world: 'when from the sameness of stimulus meanings of "Gavagai" and "Rabbit", the linguist leaps to the conclusion that a gavagai is a whole enduring rabbit, he is just taking for granted that the native is enough like us to have a brief general term for rabbits and no brief general term for rabbit stages or parts' (Quine, 1959: 464).

By doing so, the linguist would apply their own conceptual framework, mistakenly believing they have successfully determined what is in fact indeterminate or 'inscrutable': the reference of terms. Quine highlights that when translating 'gagavai' as 'rabbit' and eliminating other possibilities, such as 'undetached rabbit part', 'rabbit stage' or 'rabbit phase', the linguist is guided by an 'implicit maxim', which says that

> an enduring and relatively homogeneous object, moving as a whole against a contrasting background, is a likely reference for a short expression. If he were to become conscious of this maxim, he might celebrate it as one of the linguistic universals, or traits of all languages, and he would have no trouble pointing out its psychological plausibility. But he would be wrong; the maxim

is *his own* imposition, toward settling what is objectively indeterminate. (Quine, 1969a: 34, italics added)

Based on the evidence regarding the behaviour of speakers, linguists are unable to establish or identify unambiguously which and how many objects are actually present in the way that natives perceive reality. It is also uncertain whether their vision of the world has anything in common with that of the natives. According to Quine, this points to the need to eliminate or significantly alter the notion of reference linked to the extensional conception of meaning. Quine opts for the latter, making the notion of reference relative to a translation manual.

The ontology of a language becomes relative to the manual used by the linguist to translate into his own language. As Quine asserts, there it is possible to 'systematically reconstruct our neighbour's apparent references to rabbits as really references to rabbit stages' and reconciling 'all this with our neighbour's verbal behaviour, by cunningly readjusting our translations of his various connecting predicates so as to compensate for the switch of ontology' (Quine, 1969a: 47). This relativization becomes even more significant when we consider that sentences are not taken in isolation, but rather as part of a broader network of linguistic sentences, *holistically*. In Quine's word:

> It is to be expected that many different ways of translating ... would deliver the same empirical implications for the theory *as a whole*; deviations in the translation of one component sentence could be *compensated for in the translation* of another component sentence. Insofar, there can be no ground for saying which of two glaringly unlike translations of individual sentences is right. (Quine, 1969b: 80, italics added)

The thesis of ontological relativity is closely related to Quine's reflections on the problem of translation. There is a principle that links the concept of reference to translation: given two expressions A and B belonging, respectively, to L and to L', if B is a good translation of A, then A and B will have the same reference.

As the reference is inscrutable and relative to a translation manual, any translation produced will be *relative to a translation manual T*. Consequently, there is no single correct translation manual that aligns completely with the set of conditions C. Instead, there are *infinitely many* translation manuals that are distinct but *equally correct and legitimate*. All translation manuals can account for the empirical evidence available to linguists and the natives' dispositions to verbal behaviour. Despite being equally valid, all these manuals will be *incompatible with one another*.

This is the famous Quinean *thesis of indeterminacy of translation*, which claims that there can be different yet equally correct translation manuals with unexplained divergences, even at the level of a single sentence. In Quine's words: 'manuals for translating one language into another can be set up in divergent ways, all compatible with the totality of speech dispositions, yet incompatible with one another' (Quine, 1960: 27). Thus, indeterminacy in translation does not imply the potential for translating an expression with distinct nuances of meaning. Such options are already included in the *standard* translation manual that we use for the sake of ease, convenience, or personal preference. In Quine's view, there is no assurance that a specific translation is the sole accurate one, as it is continually possible to discover an alternative set of coherent rules for translation.

Quine attempts to address a profound philosophical issue: whether translation is possible or impossible. If the notion of meaning is indeterminate, it becomes impossible to elucidate what 'the same meaning' denotes. As Quine explains, in countless places translation manuals

> will diverge in giving, as their respective translations of a sentence of the one language, sentences of the other language which stand to each other in *no plausible sort of equivalence relation* however loose. The firmer the direct links of a sentence with non-verbal stimulation, of course, the less drastically its translations can diverge from one another from manual to manual. (Quine, 1960: 27, italics added)

Quine argues that the meaning of a sentence can only be evaluated correctly if it is understood as part of a system of coordinates in a 'background language'. In Quine's view, sentences in a language must be evaluated collectively before the 'tribunal of experience' – in other words, *holistically* – which means they need to be considered in relation to each other and to the empirical foundation.[5]

Quine compares language to a city, which has a centre and a periphery, where each sentence plays a role. The observation sentences, which are strongly linked to experience, reside in the periphery, while the standing sentences, especially those in logic and mathematics, which cannot be eliminated, are situated in the centre. Nevertheless, no sentence, not even the logical laws, can be considered entirely certain. For scientific understanding, both language and experience are essential, and one must grasp it holistically. It means that truth values are redistributed over statements, and reassessing

---

[5] 'Holistic' refers to an approach or perspective that considers the whole system, rather than focusing on individual parts, to understand and address a situation or a problem. It involves considering the interconnections and interdependencies between different elements and taking into account various factors to better understand the whole. In analytic philosophy of language, the *holistic thesis* was initially proposed by Duhem in 1906, in *La théorie physique, son objet et sa structure*, and later taken up by Quine: this is the reason why it is also named 'the Duhem-Quine thesis' (cf. Fodor & Lepore, 1992, ch. II).

one statement often leads to re-evaluating others due to logical interconnections. Quine's holistic approach to meaning is a direct consequence of his
renouncing to the two dogmas of Empiricism, largely embraced by the Vienna
Circle, as the next section aims to show. Nonetheless, Quine's holism also
presents some problems, which become more apparent within Davidson's
holistic paradigm.

4 The Notion of Synonymy and Davidson's Theory of Radical Interpretation

Quine explores different ways to define the concepts of meaning and sameness
of meaning (or synonymy), which have been vital in the definitions of translation equivalence in the history of analytic philosophy. However, Quine strongly
criticizes the notion of *synonymy*, demonstrating the difficulty of defining it
without referring to notions that are just as problematic and obscure as the
concept of meaning itself. In *Two Dogmas of Empiricism* (1953), his criticism of
the notion of synonymy brought him to abandon the notion of meaning itself,
which finally was the cause of his dramatic conclusions on radical translation.

Quine's criticism begins with the notion of analyticity,[6] by claiming that not
only is a logical truth, such as (1) 'no unmarried man is married', considered
analytic, but so is the sentence (2) 'no bachelor is married'. The issue lies in
distinguishing between analytical sentences that only contain 'logical words'
and those, such as (2), that are not logical truths but can be held true based on the
meaning of the words that make them up: 'bachelor' indeed means 'unmarried
man' in (2). Quine offers a solution to this problem by arguing that 'the
characteristic of such a statement is that it can be turned into a logical truth by
putting synonyms for synonyms; thus (2) can be turned into (1) by putting
"unmarried man" for its synonym "bachelor"' (Quine, 1953: 23, italics
added). Therefore, sentences like (2) can be considered analytic because they
are derived from logical truth, with certain expressions being substituted for
other synonymous expressions.

This definition of analyticity is nevertheless based on the notion of synonymy, though not explicitly stated. If we assume synonymy, we also assume
knowledge of what 'having the same meaning' means and thereby take the
notion of meaning itself for granted. To prevent a circular definition of

---

[6] The term 'analyticity' refers to the property of being analytic, that is, true by virtue of the meaning
of the words used. On the one hand, the term can refer to the idea that simply understanding the
meaning of a sentence is enough to know that it is true, which is known as 'epistemic analyticity'.
On the other hand, it can refer to the idea that a sentence's truth value is solely determined by its
meaning, not by facts in the world, which is known as 'metaphysical analyticity'. Quine conflated
these two readings of the term 'analyticity', leading to the assumption that they stand or fall
together (cf. Boghossian, 1997).

analyticity, we must define synonymy. We cannot 'define synonymous two expressions if the statement that asserts their equivalence is analytic' (Santambrogio, 1992: 184), as this would perpetuate the cyclical explanation of analyticity through synonymy and synonymy through analyticity.

The concept of synonymy can be better understood through *definition*. For example, the word 'bachelor' is *defined* as an 'unmarried man', as is commonly found in dictionaries. However, the definition provided by lexicographers simply assumes the synonymy identified during the research process, without actually explaining it. While definitions may include additional explanations or paraphrases to aid comprehension, they do not inherently expose the underlying synonymy, because they 'though not merely reporting a pre-existing synonymy between definiendum and definiens, do rest nevertheless on *other* pre-existing synonymies' (Quine, 1953: 25).

Quine proposes to explain synonymy through the concept of *interchangeability salva veritate* ('interchangeability preserving truth'). Translation scholars often resort to this concept in linguistics and semantics when attempting to clarify the equivalence relation in translation. They typically assume the following definition of synonymy: 'Two expressions are synonymous in a language L if and only if they may be *interchanged* in each sentence in L without altering the truth value of that sentence' (Mates, 1950: 209). As Van den Broeck (1978: 36) pointed out,

> if we take into account the fact that expressions in context not only have conceptual meanings but also convey connotative, stylistic, affective, reflected, and collocative meanings, it will in fact be difficult to discover any pair of expressions in actual speech which are really equivalent. This observation has frequently led people to declare that 'true synonyms do not exist'.

However, in *Two Dogmas of Empiricism* (1953), Quine clarifies that his attention is not on 'synonymy in the sense of complete identity in psychological associations or poetic quality; indeed no two expressions are synonymous in such a sense' (Quine, 1953: 28). Following Frege and the analytic philosophy tradition, he deals with the more restricted notion of *cognitive synonymy*, which states that two expressions are synonymous if they can be used interchangeably without changing their 'content' or truth value, but only altering their 'poetic quality' or 'psychological associations'.

Quine intends to clarify whether the concept of *interchangeability salva veritate* is robust enough to define *synonymy*, or whether some non-synonymous expressions may also be interchangeable. However, this solution poses two issues: the first being that in certain cases, two synonymous expressions cannot be exchanged without altering the truth value. For instance, in the true sentence (3) '"Bachelor" has less than ten letters', 'Bachelor' can be substituted with 'unmarried man', as follows: (4) '"Unmarried man" has less than ten letters', which is false. However, such cases might be considered insignificant as they pertain to the graphical form of the expression rather than its meaning.

Second, in order to explain synonymy using the concept of interchangeability, we require a language that is sufficiently diverse to describe potential or alternate scenarios. As Quine (1953: 31) pointed out:

> In an extensional language, therefore, interchangeability *salva veritate* is no assurance of cognitive synonymy of the desired type. That 'bachelor' and 'unmarried man' are interchangeable *salva veritate* in an extensional language assures us of no more than that is true. There is no assurance here that the extensional agreement of 'bachelor' and 'unmarried man' rests on meaning rather than merely on accidental matters of fact, as does extensional agreement of 'creature with a heart' and 'creature with a kidney'.

In other words, language needs to be able to express modalities[7] such as 'it is necessary that' or 'it is possible that'. Without such expressions, 'creature with a heart' and 'creature with a kidney' would be synonymous only because there are no creatures in our world that have a kidney but not a heart. However, if language is rich enough, 'bachelor' and 'unmarried man' can be considered synonymous expressions, while 'creature with a heart' and 'creature with a kidney' cannot be, as it is not necessarily true that creatures with a kidney also have a heart, and vice versa.

However, the concept of necessity alone is insufficient to define analyticity without the inclusion of the set of obscure intensional notions (see n. 3, Section 1, for the meaning of 'intensional' and the intensional/extensional distinction). Hence, Quine presents an alternative solution: the verification theory of meaning. As already anticipated (see Section 1 and 2), analytic philosophy has its historical origins in the Neoempiricism of the Vienna Circle, whose members believed that the meaning of a sentence can be ascertained through the method used to verify or falsify it. As Schlick explains in *Meaning and Verification* (1936):

> Thus, whenever we ask about a sentence, 'What does it mean?', what we expect is instruction as to the circumstances in which the sentence is to be used; we want a description of the conditions under which the sentence will form a *true* proposition, and of those which will make it *false*. (Schlick, 1936: 147)

In this view, synonymy is defined as follows: 'statements are synonymous if and only if they are alike in point of method of empirical confirmation or

---

[7] In general, 'modality' refers to the manner or mode in which something is done or expressed. In philosophy, modality deals with the nature and logic of possibility and necessity and it encompasses concepts such as possibility, contingency, necessity, and impossibility.

infirmation' (Quine, 1953: 37). This definition could also explain the distinction between analytic and synthetic, as we can intuitively characterize analytic sentences as those confirmed by any experience.

The theses of the verification theory of meaning are based on the dogma of reductionism, according to which 'every meaningful statement is held to be translatable into a statement (true or false) about immediate experience' (Quine, 1953: 38). However, Quine inflicted another blow to the verification theory of meaning (see also Wittgenstein's criticism in Section 2): in the Quinean perspective, individual sentences lack verification conditions since they are evaluated holistically by the 'tribunal of experience'. Thus, Quine argues that any attempts at defining the concept of analyticity ultimately fall short, either due to inadequacy or circular reasoning. The inseparable connection between analyticity and synonymy also renders the notion of meaning difficult to explain. Within the realm of analytic philosophy, other scholars, such as Davidson, have attempted to address the problem of translation equivalence by discarding intensional concepts, like meaning and sameness of meaning.

Davidson's *theory of radical interpretation* aims to reveal the translation of any given sentence, whether in any other language or in the same language in which the sentence is expressed. As Catford claimed (1965: 35), 'it is clearly necessary for translation theory to draw upon a theory of meaning'. According to Davidson, the theory of radical interpretation has to address the root of the problem of *linguistic meaning* through a 'radical' inquiry. This inquiry begins with the *fundamental question* about the semantic notion of meaning: 'What is it for words to mean what they do?' (Davidson, 1984b: xiii).

The theory that Davidson is searching for must provide a radical interpreter – someone who does not know the language nor the cultural background of the speaker – with a model to answer this question, as well as a *corpus* of information that is *necessary* and *sufficient* to understand the foreign interlocutor. According to Davidson, the theory must be *empirically verifiable* and able to offer a *holistic*, global explanation of how natural language functions:

> What is it for words to mean what they do? . . . I explore the idea that we would have an answer to this question if we knew how to construct a theory satisfying two demands: it would provide an interpretation of all utterances, actual and potential, of a speaker or group of speakers; and it would be verifiable without knowledge of the detailed propositional attitudes of the speaker. The first condition acknowledges the holistic nature of linguistic understanding. The second condition aims to prevent smuggling into the foundations of the theory concepts too closely allied to the concept of meaning. A theory that does not satisfy both conditions cannot be said to answer our opening question in a philosophically instructive way. (Davidson, 1984b: xiii)

Then it should provide an explanation for a virtually infinite number of sentences, all generated from a *finite* basic vocabulary and set of rules that can be comprehended by an interpreter with *finite* abilities. Confronted with the challenge of unlimited linguistic productivity, Davidson embraces the Fregean *principle of compositionality* as a cornerstone of his theory of meaning: a sentence's meaning is derived from its constituent parts and the rules governing how they are put together (Frege, 1884).

Davidson claims that for a theory to be able to provide an equivalent sentence *p* for any given sentence *s* in any natural language and possess such features, it must adopt *Tarski's theory of truth* as a formal model (Tarski, 1933, 1944). Therefore, Davidson accepts the concept of equivalence from Tarski's theory of truth: two sentences, *s* and *p*, are *equivalent* only when *s* is true if and only if *p* is true. For instance, '"La neve è bianca" is true in Italian only if "snow is white"' is an equivalence of the form T. Tarski's theory of truth allows for the delimitation of the extension of the truth predicate when applied to the sentences of a language (the object-language L), which is determined by the set of all T-sentences, that is, those sentences that correspond to each sentence of L and conform to the 'T-scheme':

s is T-in-L if and only if *p*

where '*s*' corresponds to the name of a declarative sentence (the same sentence with inverted commas) or to a structural description of the sentence of the object-language (L) and '*p*' to the same sentence or, if the object-language and the metalanguage (ML)[8] do not coincide, to a translation into the metalanguage, to which the term 'true' and all the other semantic notions and the T-scheme belong.

Tarski embraces the minimal requirement of any notion of truth, that is, '*the equivalence thesis*', which states that for any proposed notion of truth, each instance of the schema 's is true if and only if p' resulting from the substitution of a translation of the sentence designated by s for p is true (see Dummett, 1978; Devitt, 1984). The Tarskian model helps Davidson to give an explanation of the meaning and thus of the sameness of meaning *in terms of truth conditions*. In this way, Davidson avoids mentioning the meaning itself and sidesteps the problems already raised by Quine concerning the notions of meaning and synonymy (having the same meaning).

However, to apply Tarski's theory to natural languages, Davidson has to undertake the 'thankless work' of directing natural languages towards Tarskian formal analysis, even though they are constantly evolving and have specific

---

[8] There is a distinction between the *object-language* L, that is, the language we are talking *about*, and the *metalanguage* ML, that is, the language used to formulate the theory. The goal of this distinction is to avoid possible semantic paradoxes (for instance, the liar paradox).

syntactic-grammatical structures and indexical terms that may be contextually bound, have multiple meanings, or ambiguous meanings. Nevertheless, in *Truth and Meaning* (1967), Davidson recognizes his programme has 'a staggering list of difficulties and conundrums' (Davidson, 1984c: 35). His theory must face the problem of determining the logical form of counterfactual, causal, probabilistic sentences; adverbs, adjectives, and mass terms; sentences about beliefs, perceptions, and intentions; and action, imperative and interrogative verbs, and many others. Thus, Davidson initiated a research programme in analytic philosophy aimed at translating natural language into a formalized language based on his formal model, which made some progress: his research on performatives, adverbs, events, causal singular sentence, and quotation (Davidson, 1980a, 1984a); Burge's (1973) inquiries into proper nouns; Harman (1975) on 'ought'; and Wallace (1972) on mass terms and comparatives.

Still, one of the major limitations of the Davidsonian theory of meaning is precisely the formalization required by the Tarskian theory of truth Davidson adopted. In particular, Davidson automatically assumes the same standard first-order quantification theory as a unique resource for his theory, without justifying his choice. Davidson himself recognized that this decision was 'hasty':

> My working assumption has been that nothing more than standard first-order quantification theory is available. Indeed, I was long convinced that many alternative approaches to semantics, employing, for example, modal logics, possible world semantics, or substitutional quantification, could not be accommodated in a theory that met the demands of Convention T. I now know this was hasty. Convention T does not settle as much as I thought, and more possibilities for interesting theorizing are open than I had realized. (Davidson, 1984b: xv–xvi)

More basically, as Tarski warned, the main problem with assuming this theory of truth is that it is very doubtful that 'the language of everyday life, after being "rationalized" in this way, would still preserve its naturalness' (Tarski, 1944: 267).

5 The Principle of Charity and the Third Dogma of Empiricism

Not only Quine but also Davidson supported a holistic perspective on meaning, though reaching completely different conclusions on translation. In *Truth and Meaning* (1967), Davidson introduces his holistic view, by mentioning Frege's principle of context:

> If sentences depend for their meaning on their structure, and we understand the meaning of each item in the structure only as an abstraction from the totality of sentences in which it features, then we can give the meaning of any sentence (or word) only by giving the meaning of every sentence (and word)

in the language. Frege said that only in the context of a sentence does a word have meaning; in the same vein he might have added that only *in the context of the language* does a sentence (and therefore a word) have a meaning. (Davidson, 1984c: 22, italics added)

Davidson ties together the interpretation of sentences with the interpretation of a speaker's intentions and beliefs within a comprehensive theoretical framework. He argues that interpretation cannot start without the interpreter having some knowledge of the speaker's beliefs, as 'we cannot infer the belief without knowing the meaning, and have no chance of inferring the meaning without the belief' (Davidson, 1984e: 142). Therefore, interpretation must be approached as a comprehensive endeavour, as even the content of a single belief is dependent on its position within the broader conceptual structure that interconnects beliefs, intentions, desires, preferences, and so on.

We cannot intelligibly attribute any propositional attitude to an agent except *within the framework* of a viable theory of his beliefs, desires, intentions, and decisions. There is no assigning beliefs to a person *one by one* on the basis of his verbal behaviour, his choices, or other local signs no matter how plain and evident, for we make sense of particular beliefs only as they cohere with other beliefs, with preferences, with intentions, hopes, fears, expectations, and the rest. ... The content of a propositional attitude derives *from its place in the pattern*. (Davidson, 1980b: 221, italics added)

However, if the sentences to be interpreted are potentially infinite, there will also be an infinite number of connections, not just with an unlimited number of other sentences but also with the speaker's beliefs. As a result, the radical interpreter, who possesses finite skills, would not even be able to begin the interpretation process. Recognizing this difficulty, Davidson proposed a more tempered approach to semantic holism that reflects a 'molecular' or 'compositional' idea of meaning. According to this perspective, the meaning of a sentence is not reliant on all the sentences in a language, but solely on a *finite* number of them: 'In my view ... what one sentence means depends on the meanings of *other* sentences. I'm not an unbuttoned holist in that I do not say the meaning of a sentence depends on the meaning of *all* sentences' (Davidson, 1994a: 124).

In any case, the meaning of a sentence depends entirely on what the speaker says and the underlying beliefs implicit in their speech. However, Davidson argues that these two components, while closely related, can be separated to achieve interpretation. A distinction must be made between meaning and belief to properly assign each component. To clarify this point, Davidson discusses a variety of examples, including the following one:

If you see a ketch sailing by and your companion says, 'Look at that handsome yawl', you may be faced with a problem of interpretation. One natural possibility is that your friend has mistaken a ketch for a yawl, and has formed a false belief. But if his vision is good and his line of sight favourable it is even more plausible that he does not use the word 'yawl' quite as you do, and has made no mistake at all about the position of the jigger on the passing yacht. We do this sort of off the cuff interpretation all the time, deciding in favour of reinterpretation of words in order to preserve a reasonable theory of belief. (Davidson, 1984f: 196)

This example illustrates how the tight connection between meaning and belief in an interpretive decision can influence how a sentence is interpreted, or vice versa. Because there are so many interdependent aspects of behaviour, there is no clear-cut way to define a border between meaning and belief. In such cases, there are multiple choices available to us in interpreting what the speaker intends to convey, depending on how we disentangle the elements of belief and meaning during the interpretation process. Hence, the *indeterminacy of interpretation* is not linked to a relativistic ontological conception, as in Quine's philosophy. Instead, it is related to situations where we need to discern whether the speaker's statement is due to a mistaken belief about the world or an imperfect understanding of the meaning of the words.

This does not contradict the possibility of interpretation, because we apply the interpretative *Principle of Charity*, which involves a rational process of adjustment. According to the principle, to understand the meaning of a speaker's utterances, a radical interpreter must assume that: (a) there is a general agreement between their own beliefs and the speaker's beliefs; (b) the speaker has a set of beliefs, and most of these beliefs are coherent and true according to the interpreter's criteria for correctness; and (c) the speaker is rational from the interpreter's point of view. Evaluating the assumptions under-lying Davidson's Principle of Charity is not easy, primarily because he never provided a clearly defined single definition. He offered various formulations of the principle, emphasizing different assumptions at different times. Despite these differences, however, the assumptions of the principle are interconnected, and as a result, the various formulations cannot be regarded as different versions of the same principle, but rather as a collection of interrelated assumptions.

In his paper *Radical Interpretation* (1973), Davidson argues that in order to interpret foreign linguistic expressions, it is necessary to attribute to the speaker sentences that appear to be held true, and conditions that make those sentences correct from our perspective: 'assigning truth conditions to alien sentences that make native speakers right when plausibly possible, according, of course, to *our own view of what is right*' (Davidson, 1984d: 137, italics added). This procedure is justified by the fact that, according to the Principle of Charity, there is broad agreement between us and the speaker.

However, some scholars prefer an alternative version of the Principle of Charity, known as the *Principle of Humanity* (Grandy, 1973). This principle recommends ascribing to the speaker not necessarily what we believe to be correct, but rather what we would consider correct if we were in their position, even if they hold an irrational or bizarre idea. Compared to the Principle of Charity, the Principle of Humanity places greater emphasis on the speaker's perspective. However, both principles assume that *we* must determine what the speaker would think:

> It is of fundamental importance to make the interrelations between [the other person's beliefs and desires] *as similar as possible to our own*. If a translation tells us that the other person's beliefs and desires are connected in a way that it is *too bizarre* for us to make sense of, then the translation is useless for our purposes. So we have, as a pragmatic constrain on translation, the condition that the imputed pattern of relations among beliefs, desires and the world be *as similar to our own as possible*. (Grandy, 1973: 443, italics added)

Some authors, like Ian Hacking (1986), harshly criticized the Principles of Charity and Humanity, arguing that the silent, presupposed agreement could only be helpful for interpreting the speakers' more basic expressions. Hacking strongly objected to the formulation of these principles, asserting that it could ultimately result in a significant misinterpretation of the natives:

> To enable us to translate the speech of 'natives', may raise a wry smile. 'Charity' and 'Humanity' have long been in the missionary vanguard of colonizing Commerce. Our 'native' may be wondering whether philosophical B52s and strategic hamlets are in the offing it he will not sit up and speak like the English. Linguistic imperialism is better armed than the military for perhaps it can be proved, by a transcendental argument, that if the native does not share most of our beliefs and wants, he is just not engaged in human discourse, and is at best sub-human (The native has heard that one before too). (Hacking, 1975: 149)

Hacking's criticism does not hit the mark because the agreement presupposed by those principles is more primitive and basic than singular beliefs about everyday life. They have the transcendental nature of a common background where even cases of irrationality can be identified. Still, Hacking rightly pointed out a real risk within the analytic philosophy of language, particularly in such principles. In a form of linguistic imperialism, the interpreter's Anglophone perspective might unjustly eliminate the possibility for non-English speakers to have a different point of view. Indeed, Hacking's philosophy critiques the notion of fixed and unchanging categories shared by all human beings and highlights the dynamic nature of knowledge, language, and social practices in shaping our understanding of the world. Hacking's philosophy promotes the idea that knowledge and scientific categories are not simply objective and fixed, but they are created and shaped by human practices and language. He argues for the 'social construction of reality' (Hacking, 1999), emphasizing how our understanding of the world and our scientific concepts are influenced by specific historical, cultural, and social factors that should not be overshadowed by a single predominant system of values. Indeed, as postcolonial studies have pointed out (see e.g., Bassnett, 2013), translation might precisely highlight this imbalanced power dynamics between cultures.

Davidson at least acknowledges the potential for error when there is not a complete alignment between the interpreter's and speaker's criteria. However, this disagreement can only be comprehended within the context of the basic agreement assumed by the Principle of Charity. Thus, the margin for error is not entirely untranslatable and opaque to the interpreter, but rather a divergent perspective that can be elucidated through a broad range of shared truths: 'We make maximum sense of the words and thoughts of others when we interpret in a way that optimizes agreement (this includes room, as we said, for *explicable error*, i.e. *differences of opinion*)' (Davidson, 1984f: 197, italics added).

Therefore, according to Davidson, a situation of massive error never has to be faced because such disagreement would not be understandable or imaginable. Indeed, the Principle of Charity presupposes that other people's beliefs and behaviours are substantially similar to ours, reducing the differences among interlocutors to simple 'differences of opinion', inexactness, or explicable mistakes. Moreover, interpretations should always be evaluated by comparing them to the empirical evidence at our disposal. Indeed, as already mentioned, Davidson posits that the theory of meaning used for radical interpretation must be subjected to an empirical test in a *holistic* manner. This enables the theory to be validated in its entirety and to take into account the interconnections between various components such as sentences, beliefs, empirical data, and so on. It is due to the wide-ranging and inextricably intertwined nature of these components that Davidson asserts that interpretation theories can never have the quality of definitiveness. Thus, every interpretation has room for improvement, thereby allowing the interpreter to achieve a more complete understanding of the speaker's intentions. These considerations highlight the *conjectural and dynamical nature of interpretation*, which does not undermine the objectivity of the interpreter's comprehension.

Davidson's notion of interpretation indeterminacy differs from Quine's notion of translation indeterminacy. Quine's idea suggests the existence of different translation manuals linked to different ontologies and conceptual schemes. However, Davidson criticizes Quine's idea of a conceptual scheme and the possibility that different conceptual schemes are associated with different languages. In Davidson's view, this is a dogma, that is, the 'third dogma of Empiricism' to eliminate, which is shared by philosophers of science, historians of science, and linguists, such as Benjamin Lee Whorf, who claimed that 'we are inclined to think of language simply as a technique of expression, and not to realize that language, first of all, is a classification and arrangement of the stream of sensory experience which results in a certain world order' (Whorf, 1956: 55).

Even Kuhn (1970) used this criterion for distinguishing between conceptual schemes (and languages), albeit with some variations (Halverson, 1997). According to him, during and after a scientific revolution, it cannot be claimed that we are still using the same language, despite retaining the same terms, as the meanings of these terms change during the transition from one scientific theory to another. Such a significant shift in the organization of experience would render theories that succeed each other 'incommensurable':

> In the transition from one theory to the next words change their meanings or conditions of applicability in subtle ways. Though most of the same signs are used before and after a revolution – e.g. force, mass, element, compound, cell – the way in which some of them attach to nature has somehow changed. Successive theories are thus, we say, incommensurable. (Kuhn, 1970: 267)

Therefore, when two theories are incommensurable, they are connected with different languages and conceptual schemes. As Davidson points out, 'incommensurable' is simply a term used by Kuhn (and Feyerabend) to express 'non-intertranslatable'. Therefore, Davidson (1984f: 190) concludes that, according to Kuhn, Feyerabend, and Whorf, 'the failure of intertranslatability is a necessary condition for difference of conceptual schemes'.

In general, these scholars believed that conceptual schemes are viewed as systems of categories that belong to individuals, cultures, or even certain historical phases. They are capable of organizing the empirical content given by experience, which is neutral and uninterpreted. Different conceptual schemes have different and incompatible ways of organizing the flow of experience. Davidson believes that Quine expressed reflections that are analogous to those of Whorf and Kuhn. Indeed, Quine believed that a speaker of a language different from ours could have a conceptual scheme that is radically different from ours. Although Quine (1951) rejected the 'two dogmas of empiricism', the analytic/synthetic distinction and reductionism, he did not, according to Davidson (1984f), eliminate the *third dogma of empiricism*, which is the dualism between organizing system and something that is waiting to be organized.

In Davidson's view, it is essential to eliminate the third dogma because the notion that there could be totally different conceptual schemes organizing a neutral content and the existence of radically incommensurable languages are unacceptable. It is rather possible to undertake interlinguistic communication based on a coordinate system that is common to every language, enabling comparison. The impossibility of translating a language is contradictory to Davidson's belief that every language is a system of expression that is fundamentally *translatable* and *interpretable*. In his essay *On the Very Idea of a Conceptual Scheme* (1974), Davidson refutes the relativists' arguments by pointing out that if a language cannot be translated into another language, then it cannot truly be considered a language:

> [N]othing, it may be said, could count as evidence that some form of activity could not be interpreted in our language that was not at the same time evidence that that form of activity was not speech behaviour. If this were right ... a form of activity that cannot be interpreted as language in our language is not speech behaviour. Putting matters this way is unsatisfactory, however, for it comes to little more than making *translatability into a familiar tongue a criterion of languagehood*. As fiat, the thesis lacks the appeal of self-evidence; if it is a truth, as I think it is, it should emerge as the conclusion of an argument. (Davidson, 1984f: 185–6, italics added)

In Davidson's view, the thesis of incommensurability or incomparability of different conceptual schemes would be denied by the same metaphor of different points of view used by conceptual relativism: 'The dominant metaphor of conceptual relativism, that of differing points of view, seems to betray an underlying paradox. Different points of view make sense, but only if there is a common co-ordinate system on which to plot them; yet the existence of a common system belies the claim of dramatic incomparability' (Davidson, 1984f: 184).

As Davidson convincingly argued, we can only sensibly speak of diversity between points of view (conceptual schemes) if they can be traced back to a common coordinate system that allows for comparison. However, although these views may share some similarities, they cannot be radically different and incompatible with each other. The solution proposed by Davidson appears to avoid this paradox. Due to the principle of interpretative charity, the translation of foreign utterances occurs in a way that enables clarity of every difference – even of conceptual schemes – to emerge only against the backdrop of a massive basic agreement:

> Do we understand what we mean by a real alternative to our conceptual scheme? If a scheme could be decoded by us, then it would not, by this very token, be all that different from ours except, it might be, in ease of description

here or there. If we could explain, or describe, in a convincing way, how an alternative scheme deviates from ours, it would again be captured in our system of concepts. (Davidson, 1997: 15)

The Principle of Charity is a prerequisite not only for translation but also for identifying a language itself. If we cannot translate what a speaker says into a language we understand, we cannot recognize those sounds as a language.[9] Similarly, Jerrold Katz's *Principle of Effability* requires that there be an essential translatability between languages: 'Each proposition can be expresses by some sentence in any natural language' (Katz, 1978: 209). This principle is in turn linked to the psychological principle of expressibility: 'Each thought can be expressed by some utterance of a natural language' (Katz, 1978: 209; see also Searle, 1969, ch. 1).

Based on the fact that every human being shares the same 'inventory of possible thoughts' with others, both principles offer a radical critique of Quinean empiricism and the related theses of conceptual relativism and the indeterminacy of translation. They support the *essential intertranslatability of natural languages*. However, neither Davidson nor Katz denies the possibility of 'local' untranslatability in some cases: 'We can be clear about breakdowns in translation when they are *local* enough, for a background of generally successful translation provides what is needed to make the failures intelligible' (Davidson, 1984f: 192, italics added). However, as Katz explains, such cases cannot be traced back to the existence of different capacities for thought or language, since the failure in translation 'represents a temporary vocabulary gap (rather than a deficiency of the language) which makes it necessary to resort to paraphrase, creation of technical vocabulary, metaphorical extension, etc. in order to make translations actual in practice, as well as possible in principle' (Katz, 1978: 220).

6 Sellars and the Problem of Semantic versus Pragmatic Equivalence

The problem of translation indeterminacy, as presented by Quine, lies in the fact that there is no equivalence between sentences that are considered translations of one another. The issue of translation equivalence is a recurring concept or 'meme' in translation theory (Chesterman, 1989), and the debate surrounding this concept is highly interdisciplinary (Ervas, 2008). In translation theory, the

---

[9] In other words, but similarly, Peirce advocated for the fundamental translatability of natural languages, as he observed that 'everything may be comprehended or more strictly translated by something: that it has something which is capable of such a determination as to stand for something through this thing' (Peirce, 1865: 333).

idea of equivalence has played a crucial role in explaining the relationship between the original (source text) and the translation (target text). There is a wide range of literature on translation equivalence, which includes various viewpoints and theoretical approaches, indicating the significant role that equivalence has played in addressing translation issues (cf. Koller, 1989; Pym, 1992; Halverson, 1997; Kenny, 1998). However, defining equivalence itself is a problem that has sparked a debate without any universally accepted answers in Translation Studies and analytic philosophy.

In analytic philosophy, there has been an attempt to define translation through two primary senses of the term 'equivalence': semantic equivalence and pragmatic equivalence. The definition of translation based on *semantic equivalence* holds that given two sentences, S and S', in the natural languages L and L', respectively, S is the translation of S' if they have the same meaning. On the other hand, the definition of translation based on *pragmatic equivalence* states that S is the translation of S' if they have the same function or role in L and L'. The concept of pragmatic equivalence was introduced by Sellars in 1963 and later adopted by Davidson in 1986. From this perspective, as pointed out (Marconi, 2010), differences in communicative content are not considered differences in meaning, but instead as differences in tone. For instance, if one considers the two sentences (1) 'Francesca has not *yet* gone to Paris', and (2) 'Francesca has not gone to Paris', they differ in their overall communicative content, because (1) contains the word 'yet', but not (2) suggests that Francesca is expected to go to Paris. Thus, (1) and (2) are semantically equivalent, but they are not pragmatically equivalent, because the role of the word 'yet' in (1), conveying the communicative effect of an expectation, is missing in (2).

One could reformulate the definition of translation based on the concept of semantic equivalence, according to the theory proposed by Davidson (1984a): S translates S' if they have the same truth conditions. The Davidsonian theory of radical interpretation, which uses Tarski's theory of truth as a formal model (Tarski, 1933, 1944), could allow us to assign to each sentence of a given language on the left side of a biconditional its translation into another language on the right side of the biconditional. This definition of translation presents various problems, including the lack of consideration for differences in tone and pragmatic nuances, which are often essential in conveying the intended message. In contrast, Sellars' definition of translation, which is based on the concept of pragmatic equivalence, offers a more comprehensive understanding that takes into account such differences to effectively preserve the overall communicative content.

By focusing on the role that an expression plays in its respective linguistic system rather than its specific meaning, we can better assess how well it functions within a given context. For example, the French expression 'À tout à l'heure' may be considered a good translation of the English expression 'See you later' in a particular situation, despite the fact that they do not share the same truth conditions. However, while pragmatic equivalence can be an effective tool for understanding the role of expressions within language systems, it should be recognized that this correspondence is primarily a matter of use and context rather than exact definition. In Sellars' words, it is 'a correspondence of *use*, or, as I prefer to say, role. Linguistic roles and role aspects differ in kind and complexity. Rarely does an expression in one language play exactly the same role as an expression in another' (Sellars, 1963: 203).

Furthermore, there are many instances of language use where it may not be clear whether a sentence has truth conditions or what they are. For example, the English sentence 'See you later' could be translated not only from the French expression 'À tout à l'heure' but also from the French expression 'À bientôt', if the same person will not be seen again that day. Therefore, the use of 'See you later' and 'À tout à l'heure' is not entirely equivalent because 'See you later' could be used in situations where 'À tout à l'heure' would not be used. However, the two expressions could be considered partially equivalent or to possess some degree of pragmatic equivalence. The translator should identify the context in which the French translation 'À tout à l'heure' is more appropriate than 'À bientôt', taking into account the expectations of a French reader in that context. As Sellars (1963: 203) points out: 'There are degrees of likeness of meaning, and meaning statements are to be construed as having a tacit reader to the effect that the correspondence is in a relevant respect and obtains to a relevant degree.' From this point of view, the notion of pragmatic equivalence would not be empty, but vague.

The pragmatic equivalence between expressions is never absolute, but instead presents a certain degree of variation depending on the context of utterance. Other factors may also contribute to the overall meaning of the expression that was uttered: 'Equivalence does not allow itself to be defined ... in a static way; it isn't – in a given couple of languages – absolute; it is to be established only in relation to many values which influence the translation process in a different *hierarchy* every time' (Reiss & Vermeer, 1984: 165, italics added). From context to context, the translator should establish a 'hierarchy of equivalences' that contribute to the translation process. Pragmatic equivalence is, therefore, not a static concept but a process that takes into account the different values of an utterance such as its prosodic characteristics, tone, and so on, and the multiple variables of the context in which it is expressed.

These observations do not differ much from Davidson's considerations in *A Nice Derangement of Epitaphs* (1986) on the need to modify our theory in real-time communication to optimize understanding between the interpreter and the speaker. In fact, during communicative encounters, our own hypotheses on translation equivalence, our intuitions on the intentions of others, and our developing linguistic skills lead us to make thoughts expressed by our interlocutor 'commensurable'. The pragmatic equivalence approach to translation aims specifically to capture how, in a given context, an utterance manages to have the same communicative effect intended by the speaker who initially uttered it. In concrete cases of communication, the conceptual node of equivalence does not refer to a static relationship between utterances but rather transforms into a dynamic process that unfolds over time. Equivalence becomes a transitory and ever-changing agreement between the interpreter and the speaker, shaped by the speaker's evolving meaning and interpretations.

Although Davidson began by grounding his own theory of meaning on Tarskian theory of truth, he has progressively 'liberalized' the criterion of equivalence, which, in his opinion, forms the basis of both translation and interpretation. Davidson's explanation of equivalence is no longer based on the sameness of meaning of the expression or their truth conditions, as every triangular relationship among the speaker, interpreter, and communicative context is unique and continuously changing. As Malmkjær notes (1993: 141), comparing the 'second' Davidson and Toury,

> Davidson's account is not given in terms of the meaning of expressions being the same. Meaning is seen as a relationship between an utterance, a speaker, a time, a set of circumstances and a hearer. Each such relationship is unique. A unique relationship cannot be replicated. Therefore, we can forget about defining equivalence in terms of 'meaning'. Rather, there are, as Toury, says, possible equivalents, i.e. those terms or utterances which we might have used in those circumstances, as well as actual equivalents, i.e. the terms actually used in a translation.

In *A Nice Derangement of Epitaphs* (1986), Davidson revisits his own criterion of translatability. He no longer sees it as concerning an abstract relationship between languages, implying some sort of 'symmetry' between them. Rather, he precisely describes the search for equivalence as an attempt to continuously apply our expectations in each communicative encounter in response to incoming information. The aim is to achieve a concrete agreement with our interlocutor through translation. Later, in his paper *James Joyce and Humpty Dumpty* (1989), Davidson employs this new concept of translation equivalence in analysing the relationship between writer, text, and reader (translator) in a single text, as well as in different texts linked by Joyce's writing.

Davidson (1986: 441) attempts to explain 'how people, who already have a language ..., manage to apply their skill or knowledge to *actual cases of interpretation*'. Davidson primarily refers to cases where speakers share the same mother tongue. In these instances, he argues that an interpreter can interpret utterances of sentences they have never before encountered by using a theory of meaning that is modelled on Tarski's theory of truth, and thus maintains the same limitations previously pointed out (see Section 4). Davidson now compares this theory to a 'machine' that is available to the interpreter, which can generate interpretations of sentences based on a finite basic vocabulary and a finite set of composition rules. This 'machine' makes language a

> *complex abstract object*, defined by giving a finite list of expressions (words), rules for constructing meaningful concatenations of expressions (sentences), and a semantic interpretation of the meaningful expressions based on seman-tic features of individual words. ... We tend to forget that there are no such things in the world; there are only people and their various written and acoustical products. (Davidson, 1992: 107–8)

Now Davidson admits that we never need such a language in our everyday communication with others, but it could be interesting only to philosophers, psychologists, and linguists. We can simply understand what other people tell us, and we can manage to be understood without relying on such an unobservable and unchangeable 'object'. Davidson (1994b: 2) concludes 'there is no such thing as what some philosophers (me included) have *called* a language'. He is questioning the conventional view of language that he had shared for quite some time with the majority of linguists and philosophers of language. Currently, he is keener on exploring occurrences such as *lapsus linguae* ('slip of the tongue') and malaprop-isms, which standard depictions of linguistic competence do not account for. Davidson believes that these occurrences are inadequate when it comes to explain-ing how our communication is successful, despite their existence.

Davidson argues that interpreters rely on a *prior theory*, which is still based on Tarski's model, to interpret speakers. This theory reflects their previous knowledge about how to interpret the speaker in question. This initial know-ledge is based on limited information about the speaker's appearance and behaviour, as well as any deeper knowledge she may have. As such, there are countless prior theories based on individual speakers and the interpreter's level of familiarity with their customs, background, and situation. As the interpreter processes new information, the interpreter may adjust the initial theory to create a more accurate interpretation, referred to as a *passing theory*. Davidson cites the example of Mrs. Malaprop, whose use of the phrase 'a nice derangement of epitaphs' actually meant 'a nice arrangement of epithets'. In this case, the interpreter must develop a new theory to assign new meanings to the words 'derangement' and 'epitaph'.

As the interpreters use a provisional theory to comprehend the speakers, they cannot be sure if this theory's adaptation will be effective for all of the speakers' future statements. Indeed, a passing theory tells us only how we have to 'interpret a particular utterance on a particular occasion' (Davidson, 1986: 443). The prior theory will undergo constant modifications as new theories emerge, and with continuous comparison to the speakers, it will be enhanced. Ultimately, the interpreter will gain a better understanding of the speakers by progressively adjusting their own theories.

Thus, Davidson highlights the creativity of interpreters, asserting that it cannot be explained by a description of linguistic competence as a limited set of rules, conventions, or applications determined by history and linguistic practices. Instead, Davidson aims to disregard such explanations to emphasize the significant role of creativity in language use (for criticism, see Rawling, 2023). Davidson believes that the flexible accommodation of prior theories and the use of passing theories to comprehend speakers' utterances characterize not only situations regarding *lapsus linguae* or malapropisms but also all types of interpretation. This is because phenomena such as *lapsus linguae* and malapropisms are 'omnipresent and pervasive' (Davidson, 1986: 433). Therefore, every form of communication needs to accommodate prior theories and undergo constant changes in passing theories. Though conventions, shared practices, and uses may facilitate understanding, it is ultimately the *creative dimension* of our linguistic use that drives successful interpretation.

However, as Ian Hacking (1986) and Michael Dummett (1986) rightly warned, linguistic phenomena such as *lapsus linguae* or malapropisms do not seem omnipresent; they usually are considered exceptional cases in our usual way of communicating. Generally, speakers accurately convey their intended message without confusion. Thus, we cannot dismiss linguistic rules and conventions entirely simply because these errors are anomalies rather than the norm. In Dummett's words (1986: 474), the conventions 'are what constitute a social practice; to repudiate the role of convention is to deny that a language is in this sense a practice. In the exceptional cases ... there are indeed no rules to follow: that is what makes such cases *exceptional*'.

On the contrary, Davidson emphasizes the creative and productive power of language, giving Joyce's use of language as an example in the paper *James Joyce and Humpty Dumpty* (1989). Joyce does not abandon his nationality, religion, and language to annihilate it; rather, he recreates it, putting his reader 'in the situation of the jungle linguist trying to get the hang of a new language and a novel culture' (Davidson, 1991: 11). The 'radical reader' of Joyce's works understands the meaning of his writing, despite being outside the conventions and rules of their society and language. However, it could also be argued that

Joyce's non-conventional style of writing is an exceptional case, rather than an ordinary mode of communication. It is challenging to grasp how an interpreter can comprehend the speaker without any rules, conventions, or social practices in place.

However, Davidson does not believe that Joyce's language is completely disconnected from any context, despite being created from scratch. Davidson holds a different view from Humpty Dumpty, who stated: 'When *I* use a word it means just what I choose it to mean' (Davidson, 1991: 1), because he does not believe in the existence of a private language. As Wittgenstein claimed (PI, 243–71), without sharing one's own language with somebody, the speaker could not know in any way what the correct language use is. Instead, the language created by Joyce is intersubjective, and – however detached from rules and conventions it may be – it opens 'a hermeneutic space between the reader and the text' (Davidson, 1991: 12).

7 Grice and the Translation of Implicit Meaning

Analytic philosophers like Frege, Russell, and Carnap, who worked in Europe, as well as analytic philosophers like Quine and Davidson, who worked in the United States, belong to the school of thought known as 'the philosophy of ideal language'. The philosophy of ideal language posits that language can be perfected to accurately and precisely represent reality. Ideal language philosophers believe that language can be made logical, unambiguous, and objective by creating a perfect language that is free of the ambiguities and limitations of natural language. As already pointed out (see Sections 1 and 2), the goal of the philosophy of ideal language is to create a language that is perfectly suited for scientific discourse and mathematical calculations, free from the limitations of natural language. Translation presents a challenge for philosophers of ideal language, who must consider the structural variances and multiple meanings found in natural languages, a task that proves difficult to accomplish through formalized languages.

The philosophy of ordinary language is instead a philosophical approach that emphasizes the importance of analysing language as it is actually used in everyday contexts, rather than relying on abstract or formal definitions. It seeks to uncover the implicit assumptions and connotations that are embedded in everyday language, and to use this understanding to shed light on philosophical problems and debates. Therefore, the examples provided by ordinary language philosophers are not formalization or regimentation of pieces of language, nor artificial mental experiments, but rather utterances of everyday conversations. Thus, the work of philosophers of ordinary language, such as John Austin and Paul Grice, is very relevant to under-standing translation, focusing on 'the way utterances are used in communi-cative situations and the way we interpret them in context' (Baker, 1992: 217). Austin (1962) took concepts from Frege such as tone and speech act force, making them fundamental to the speech act theory; Grice (1989) highlighted the importance of the speaker's intention in understanding meaning in conversational contexts.

Although Davidson acknowledged the importance of speakers' intentions in conversational contexts as part of the holistic interpretive project, he did not assign them the same weight as Grice did in his philosophy. Grice considered interpretation to be an inferential process that is guided by both the conventional and intended meanings (Grice, 1989). According to Grice, the interpreter expects that the speaker's utterance adheres to certain basic standards of rationality, as expressed in the Cooperative Principle: 'Make your conversa-tional contribution such as is required, at the stage at which it occurs, by the accepted purpose or direction of the talk exchange in which you are engaged' (Grice, 1975: 45). Grice's Cooperative Principle emphasizes that the interpreter must understand a specific person in a particular conversational context. Therefore, interpretation cannot be a generalized approach, but rather should focus on certain aspects of the speaker's behaviour in a specific conversational situation.

While the Principle of Charity does not offer a means to discern conversa-tional moves that may appear irrational, deviant, or inappropriate within a given context, the Cooperative Principle elucidates how speakers can express one thing and still be rightfully comprehended as intending to convey something else. The Cooperative Principle is indeed the basis for the Gricean famous Conversational Maxims, divided into the four Kantian categories: 'Quantity, Quality, Relation, and Manner' (Grice, 1989: 26). The categories, along with their maxims, are the following:

Quantity
1. Make your contribution as informative as is required (for the current pur-poses of the exchange).
2. Do not make your contribution more informative than is required.

Quality: "Try to make your contribution one that is true"
1. Do not say what you believe to be false.
2. Do not say that for which you lack adequate evidence.

Relation
1. Be relevant

Manner: Be perspicuous
1. Avoid obscurity of expression
2. Avoid ambiguity
3. Be brief (avoid unnecessary prolixity)
4. Be orderly (Grice, 1989: 26–7)

A *conversational implicature* arises when the Cooperative Principle and Conversational Maxims are deliberately violated. It can be calculated on the basis of the conventional meaning of the expression used, the conversational maxims, and specific contextual information coming from the conversational context. As Grice pointed out (Grice, 1989: 28), 'there are of course all sorts of other maxims (aesthetic, social, or moral in character), such as "Be polite", that are also normally observed by participants in talk exchanges, and these may also generate nonconventional implicatures'. Conversational Maxims are considered universal in conversations. However, the latest maxims, such as the maxim of politeness, can vary from culture to culture, making them essential in translation.

The Cooperative Principle is integral to the broader Gricean theory of rationality (Grice, 2001), where human rationality manifests in an interpreter's drive to explain a speaker's actions – be they verbal or non-verbal. The Gricean theory of meaning aims to explain how a speaker can say something while meaning something else in a specific conversational context (Holdcroft, 1981; Atlas, 2005) instead. To achieve this, Grice provides an account of the interpretation of the speaker's linguistic behaviour that would be otherwise considered irrational. The Gricean theory does provide a way to understand how people can exhibit irrational linguistic behaviour and still be interpreted as conveying meaningful messages. The concept of *implicature*, in particular, is employed to account for how the meaning of a sentence may deviate from its conventional meaning – that is, the meaning derived from the composition of the conventional meanings of its individual components – and still be coherent (Avramides, 1989).

Unlike Quine, Grice does not reject the notion of conventional meaning. In a paper co-authored with Peter Strawson and titled *In Defense of a Dogma* (1956), Grice defended the notion of meaning against Quine's criticisms in *Two Dogmas of Empiricism* (1953). Grice and Strawson argued that it is reasonable to discuss sentence translation because the concept of meaning is meaningful.

> For we frequently talk of the presence or absence of relations of synonymy between kinds of expressions – e.g., conjunctions, particles of many kinds, whole sentences – where there does not appear to be any obvious substitute for the ordinary notion of synonymy, in the way in which coextensionality is

said to be a substitute for synonymy of predicates. Is all such talk meaningless? Is all talk of correct or incorrect *translation* of sentences of one language
into sentences of another meaningless? It is hard to believe that it is. But if we
do successfully make the effort to believe it, we have still harder renunci-
ations before us. If talk of sentence-synonymy is meaningless, then it seems
that talk of sentences having a meaning at all must be meaningless too. For if
it made sense to talk of a sentence having a meaning, or meaning something,
then presumably it would make sense to ask 'What does it mean?' And if it
made sense to ask 'What does it mean?' of a sentence, then sentence-
synonymy could be roughly defined as follows: Two sentences are synonymous if and only if any true answer to the question 'What does it mean?' asked
of one of them, is a true answer to the same question, asked of the other.
(Grice & Strawson, 1956: 146)

However, while never questioning conventional meaning, Grice dedicates his
work to the notion of *speaker's meaning*, that is, the intended meaning of the
speaker or the implicit meaning of the utterance, which provides a key to
understanding irrationality in the speaker's linguistic behaviour. However,
implicatures, especially due to the vague nature of the *implicatum* ('that
which is implied'), require a more fundamental rule for rationality to be effective in specific conversational contexts. In Grice's words:

> The following may provide a first approximation to a general principle. Our
> talk exchanges do not normally consist of a succession of disconnected
> remarks, and would not be rational if they did. They are characteristically,
> to some degree at least, cooperative efforts; and each participant recognizes in
> them, to some extent, a common purpose or set of purposes, or at least
> a mutually accepted direction. (Grice, 1989: 26)

Here, Grice makes it clear that his theory of conversation requires a foundation,
namely that there exists an implicit common purpose or agreed-upon direction
in conversation, which determines the attribution of rationality. This foundation
is provided by the Cooperative Principle.

It is crucial to point out that Grice presents the Cooperative Principle as
a normative definition of conversation, and that it can be violated, without
'destroying the foundation of intelligibility on which all interpretation rests'
(Davidson, 1990: 320), as in the case of the Davidsonian Principle of Charity.
When compared to the Principle of Charity, the Cooperative Principle seems
more like a regulative norm suggesting that participants should work towards
a shared goal. The Cooperative Principle is a 'rough general principle which
participants will be expected (*ceteris paribus*) to observe' (Grice, 1989: 26), but
they are not obliged to follow it. Instead, the speaker often violates it, thereby
giving rise to an implicature. The cooperative interpreter, who trusts the
speaker's cooperative rational behaviour in communicating their thoughts,

should infer what the speaker intended to say and thereby grasp the conversational implicature. This is one of the most exploited Gricean ideas: conversational implicatures are generally considered to be a part of the meaning that is not literally expressed, but rather implicated and implicitly communicated in a conversational context.

It has been argued that the relationship between the Cooperative Principle and the Conversational Maxims is problematic, as it provides no concrete method for applying the general principle to specific cases of conversational practice (Kasher, 1976; Leech, 1983; Levinson, 1983). However, the Gricean Conversational Maxims aim to explain when and how the Cooperative Principle can be violated, unlike the Davidsonian Principle of Charity. While the Principle of Charity is a constitutive condition for interpreting the speaker and cannot be broken, the Cooperative Principle is regulative. If a speaker violates it or its Maxims, communication does not necessarily fail. Grice intended to treat talking as a type of purposive and rational behaviour. If the Cooperative Principle is violated, the interpreter uses inferential reasoning to grasp the intended meaning, which explains the speaker's linguistic behaviour in a rational way. Therefore, from this perspective, the Gricean Cooperative Principle proves more 'charitable' than the Davidsonian Principle of Charity. In summary, although some scholars have challenged the connection between the Cooperative Principle and the Conversational Maxims, Grice's approach to communication as rational behaviour provides a satisfactory explanation of how the Cooperative Principle can be violated and still enable fruitful communication via implicit meaning.

The implicit meaning can be preserved in translation (Ervas, 2022), for instance in the following case of generalized (1) and particularized (2) conversational implicatures (Grice, 1975: 51) translated into Italian (a) and French (b):

(1)   Michele made dinner *and* took a shower.
    (a) Michele preparò la cena *e* fece una doccia.
    [Michele made dinner and took a shower.]
    (b) Michele prépara le dîner *et* prit une douche.[10]
    [Michele made dinner and took a shower.]

(2) A: Smith does not seem to have a girlfriend these days.
    B: He has been paying a lot of visits to New York lately.

---

[10] Here we are preserving the same proper name in the translations, but for the problem of translating proper names, see Burgess, 2005; Felappi & Santambrogio, 2019.

(a) A: Smith   non sembra avere una ragazza in questi giorni.
        [Smith does not seem to have a girlfriend   these days.]
    B: Ultimamente ha fatto   molte visite a New York.
        [lately (he) has been paying a lot of visits to New York.]
(b) A: Smith ne   semble pas avoir de petite amie ces jours-ci.
        [Smith does not seem to   have a girlfriend   these days.]
    B: Il a effectué de nombreuses visites à New York ces derniers temps.
        [He has been paying a lot of visits to New York lately].

In the first case, the temporal sequence conveyed by using 'and' in a list of events is maintained through the translation of 'and' to 'e' in Italian and 'et' in French. In the second case, if the conversational context remains the same, the implicature that Smith has a girlfriend is preserved in the Italian and French translations. This is because conversational implicatures are generally *non-detachable*, meaning that no matter which way the proposition is expressed it will give rise to the same implicatures. If we use the translated sentence with the same propositional content and in the same circumstances as the original sentence, the same implicature will follow.

Following Grice, the current debate in analytic philosophy of language continues to revolve around his three main conceptual contributions: (a) the notion of communication as an expression of the speaker's intentions, (b) the existence of an implicitly shared cooperative behaviour guided by rational standards articulated by the Principle of Cooperation and Conversational Maxims, and (c) the differentiation between what the speaker said and what the speaker meant. Contemporary scholars studying non-literal language understanding have challenged Grice's philosophy,[11] questioning the notion of a clear-cut distinction between literal or conventionally encoded meaning and non-literal or implied meaning. From a Gricean perspective, what is explicitly said comes from a sentence's conventional meaning, and the Conversational Maxims' role pertains only to the realm of implicit communication.

For example, Grice's pragmatic characterizations of metaphor (1989) – as well as the work of John Searle (1993) – 'assume that there is a clear, sharp notion of sentence-meaning, or what is said by a sentence, that contrasts with what it can be used to mean' (Stern, 2006: 244). Claudia Bianchi argued that Grice's approach still maintains the idea of a conventional, linguistically

---

[11] Challengers include both neo-Gricean scholars, such as Jay Atlas (2005), Laurence Horn (2006), and Stephen Levinson (2000), aiming to revise the Gricean theory of meaning, and post-Gricean scholars, such as François Récanati (2004), Kent Bach (1994), and Dan Sperber and Deirdre Wilson (1986/1995), aiming to propose alternative theories to the Gricean theory of meaning.

encoded meaning: 'Grice, even though intending to unhinge the traditional view of language as proposed by the code model, provided instead the theoretical tools to defend it' (Bianchi, 2009: 74). This is precisely how Grice links the interpretation of the speaker's meaning to a shared conventional meaning and context-specific knowledge that is mutually understood by both the speaker and interpreter.

8 Kripke's Translation Test

In analytic philosophy, translation has also been used as a *test* to identify lexically ambiguous words (Zwicky & Sadock, 1975; Hirst, 1987). If a sentence cannot be translated in a word-to-word fashion, this serves as evidence for a real ambiguity in the original sentence's meaning. Kripke (1979) expanded this method to identify any ambiguity in semantics or syntax. He distinguished between what words represent and what the speaker conveys by utilizing them in a particular context, following Grice (1975). For instance, the sentence 'Where is the bank?' might carry different meanings in diverse contexts, but it is a matter of discrepancies in the words' meaning, not in the speaker's meaning. On the other hand, sentences containing definite descriptions, such as 'The murderer of Smith is insane', display a dichotomy between referential and attributive use regarding what the speaker is trying to convey. In Kripke's view, it is unreasonable to expect alternative translations into other languages disambiguating the referential and the attributive readings of the definite description 'The murderer of Smith', because such readings concern pragmatic uses of language rather than linguistically encoded senses.

Kripke's paper titled *Speaker's Reference and Semantic Reference* (1979) delved into the concept of definite descriptions, referring to the use of 'the' to denote a particular individual, as demonstrated in the oft-cited example of 'The murderer of Smith'. The paper specifically examined Keith Donnellan's distinction between *attributive and referential uses of definite descriptions*:

> A speaker who uses a definite description attributively in an assertion, states something about whoever or whatever is the so-and-so. A speaker who uses a definite description referentially in an assertion, on the other hand, uses the description to enable his audience to pick out whom or what he is talking about and states something about that person or thing. (Donnellan, 1966: 285)

When the phrase 'The murderer of Smith' is used in the sentence 'The murderer of Smith is insane', it can be used attributively to refer to the brutal killing without identifying a specific person, or referentially to identify a specific person such as Jones. The proper name could actually replace the definite description in referential use, but not in attributive use where the speaker may not know who the referent is. Donnellan thinks that the distinction between the attributive and referential use of definite description is pragmatic, rather than semantic: it is 'a *function of the speaker's intentions* in a particular case' (Donnellan, 1996: 297): He further claimed that there is no ambiguity in the meaning of words between the referential and the attributive readings of definite descriptions, but rather a pragmatic ambiguity:

> 'The murderer of Smith' may be used either way in the sentence 'The murderer of Smith is insane'. It does not appear plausible to account for this, either, as an ambiguity in the sentence. The grammatical structure of the sentence seems to me to be the same whether the description is used referentially or attributively: that is, it is not syntactically ambiguous. Nor does it seem at all attractive to suppose an ambiguity in the meaning of the words; it does not appear to be semantically ambiguous. (Perhaps we could say that the sentence is pragmatically ambiguous: the distinction between roles that the description plays is a function of the speaker's intentions.) These, of course, are intuitions; I do not have an argument for these conclusions. Nevertheless, the burden of proof is surely on the other side. (Donnellan, 1966: 297)

Kripke bore the responsibility of providing evidence and asserted that there is no reason for assuming a pragmatic ambiguity, as it is 'not "uses", in some pragmatic sense, but *senses* of a sentence which can be analyzed' (Kripke, 1979: 13). Based on Grice's (1975) ideas, Kripke made a distinction between the meaning of a speaker's words in a specific situation and what the speaker intended by using those words in that situation. Consider the sentence 'She asked me where the bank is' as an example: depending on the context, it could refer to a financial institution or a riverbank, but this ambiguity is a matter of word meaning, not speaker intent. This type of semantic ambiguity may not exist in other languages, as different languages may use different words for distinct meanings. Indeed, 'there is no reason for the ambiguity to be preserved in languages unrelated to our own' (Kripke, 1979: 19).

However, the speaker's meaning is shaped by contextual factors and her own intentions, rather than linguistic convention. Consider the sentence '*The murderer of Smith* is insane': the difference between the referential and the attributive use of the definite description is based on the speaker's meaning, not on words' meaning. Thus, we should not expect to find another language having different words for different uses of definite descriptions: 'if the sentence is not (syntactically or) semantically ambiguous, it has only *one* analysis; to say that it has two distinct analyses is to attribute a syntactic or semantic ambiguity to it' (Kripke, 1979: 13).

It is unlikely that a D-language (i.e., a 'Donellan's unambiguous language') would have different words for attributive and referential uses of definite descriptions, such as 'the' and 'ze', as a unitary interpretation of definite descriptions based on the speaker's meaning can be provided. According to Kripke, assuming pragmatic ambiguity without necessity is considered the 'lazy man's approach' in philosophy. Kripke encourages philosophers to avoid positing multiple senses or ambiguities where a unitary interpretation is possible. Kripke proposes a unitary explanation for attributive and referential uses of definite descriptions based on the speaker's general and specific intentions. In referential use, the speaker has a general intention to refer to an object. In attributive use, the speaker has a specific intention to refer to the object on a certain occasion. Sometimes, the referential and attributive uses can overlap, such as when the specific intention is simply to refer to the object that the speaker has in mind.

Additionally, Kripke suggested an empirical method, a 'translation test', to determine if a real meaning ambiguity exists in the original statement: 'We can ask empirically whether languages are in fact found that contain distinct words expressing the allegedly distinct senses. If no such language is found, once again this is evidence that a unitary account of the word or phrase in question should be sought' (Kripke, 1979: 19). Kripke himself provided the example of the word 'know', which can be disambiguated via translation into other languages, as for instance into Italian: 'conoscere' and 'sapere'. In his view, the failure of one-to-one translatability would prove the existence of a genuine ambiguity in the meaning encoded in the original sentence.

Thus, Kripke proposed the 'translation test' to check if there is a genuine semantic ambiguity in the original statement: this involves examining if there are languages where different words exist to express the supposedly different meanings. If no such language is found, it supports the idea that a single pragmatic explanation for the word or phrase in question should be pursued. However, the test of translation was unsuccessful in detecting instances of words that are lexically ambiguous or homonymous, which possess different but unrelated meanings (Zwicky & Sadock, 1975; Hirst, 1987). Indeed, as previously noted (Ervas, 2014), translation into other languages can also clarify the meanings of polysemous words, which have multiple but related meanings. For instance, the Italian sentence

'Era il   *nipote*   di Lussu'
[(He) was the grandson/nephew Lussu's]

can be translated into English as either

'He was Lussu's *grandson*',

or

'He was Lussu's *nephew*',

depending on the family relationship between Lussu and the subject of the sentence. It does not follow from the existence of these alternative translations that the Italian word 'nipote' is lexically ambiguous.

Despite cautioning against relying too heavily on the 'translation test', Kripke advised that it still requires more thorough examination and improvement:

> The mere fact that some language subdivides the extension of an English word into several subclasses, with their own separate words, and has no word for the whole extension, does not show that the English word was ambiguous (think of the story that the Eskimos have different words for different kinds of snow). If many unrelated languages preserve a single word, this in itself is evidence for a unitary concept. On the other hand, a word may have different senses that are obviously related. One sense may be metaphorical for another (though in that case, it may not really be a separate sense, but simply a common metaphor). 'Statistics' can mean both statistical data and the science of evaluating such data. And the like. (Kripke, 1979: 26 fn. 29)

The purpose of the 'translation test' was to discover different translations into another language that would differentiate the meanings of an original sentence. This test aimed to demonstrate that the original sentence had true semantic ambiguity. Kripke, who shared Grice's view, disagreed with Donnellan's opinion that two alternative translations in different languages could clarify the referential or attributive uses of definite descriptions. In the article *L'irrimediabile dilemma del traduttore* (*The Translator's Irredeemable Dilemma*, 2009), Alberto Voltolini proposed a strengthened version of Kripke's 'translation test'. Voltolini claimed that this test could be used to identify any truly semantic phenomenon in the original sentence:

> Any phenomenon of signification indifferent to translation is pragmatic, while any phenomenon of signification that not only is pointed out by a difference in translation as Kripke argues, but even forces a choice between a translation that preserves it and one which does not preserve it, is semantic. Translation assumes therefore the value of test or identification criterion of a phenomenon of signification as a genuine semantic phenomenon. (Voltolini, 2009: 45)

Voltolini built on Kripke's work by suggesting that translation can be used to verify the presence of genuinely semantic phenomena in a given text. This is accomplished through the identification of multiple analyses that could be represented by different senses in another language. When a translator is presented with two or more possible translations of the same sentence, this indicates a genuine semantic phenomenon in the original text. Voltolini extended Kripke's approach by suggesting that translation can also differentiate between semantic and pragmatic phenomena by revealing divergent senses expressed through different words in the target language.

One example of this is when a translator is required to assign a reference, which involves selecting between different translations of a sentence, much like what occurs during lexical disambiguation. An illustration of this is provided by Katz (1978: 222) in the potential translations of the sentence

'He thinks that he wins'

into the Hopi language:

(a) Pam navoti:ta (pam) mo:titani-qate;
   [he   thinks   (he)   win   – =]
(b) Pam navoti:ta (pam) mo:titani-q.
   [he   thinks   (he)   win   – ≠]

Translation (a) conveys a co-referential relationship, whereas translation (b) fails to maintain this relationship. This is because the subject of the verb 'thinks' in the translated sentence does not refer to the same entity as the subject of the verb 'wins'. The Hopi language does possess adequate linguistic resources for resolving co-reference.

In his work, Voltolini (2009) presented several examples highlighting situations in which the translator may have to decide between alternative translations that maintain certain aspects of the sentence's meaning while sacrificing others. One common difficulty faced by translators is choosing between a translation that preserves the sentence's linguistic meaning but neglects the use of wordplay and a translation that maintains the wordplay but deviates from the linguistic meaning. For instance, Voltolini (2009: 35) provided an example in which the Italian translation of the German sentence

     '*Weiche*,   Wotan,   *Weiche*!' (R. Wagner, *Rheingold*)
[Give way/Soft-boiled, Wotan, Give way/Soft-boiled!]

presents the translator with various alternatives:

(a) Vattene,   Wotan, vattene!;
   [Give way, Wotan, Give way!]
(b) Alla coque,   Wotan, alla coque!;
   [Soft-boiled, Wotan, Soft-boiled!]
(c) *Marcia*,   Wotan, *marcia*!
   [March/rotten, Wotan, March/rotten!]

Translations (a) and (b) retain the linguistic meaning in Italian, distinguishing between two possible interpretations ('vattene' applied to a person, and 'alla coque' applied to eggs) but fail to capture the pun in the original German sentence. Translation (c) preserves the pun, as the Italian word 'marcia' can mean both the imperative verb 'march' and the feminine adjective 'rotten', but at the expense of losing the linguistic meaning of the German word 'Weiche'.

It is worth noting that loss in translation, as argued by Voltolini (2009: 41–4), is not a result of mere linguistic differences between languages, but instead it is necessary in translation. For instance, when moving from *oratio obliqua* ('reported speech') to *oractio recta* ('direct speech'), the translator cannot retain both the original sentence's reference and its truth value (T, true; F, false), as in the following example:

(*oratio obliqua*):
'Francesca says that Ichnusa beer, like Socrates, makes you say what it wants'

(a) 'Francesca dice che la birra Ichnusa, come Socrate, ti   fa   dire ciò che vuole'.
[Francesca says that beer Ichnusa, like Socrates, you makes say what (it) wants]

(b) 'Francesca dit que la bière Ichnusa, comme Socrate, te   fait   dire ce qu'elle veut'.
[Francesca says that beer Ichnusa, like Socrates,   you makes say what (it) wants]

(*oratio recta*):
'Francesca says: "Ichnusa beer, like Socrates, makes you say what it wants"'

(a) 'Francesca dice: "La birra Ichnusa, come Socrate, ti   fa   dire ciò che vuole"' (F)
[Francesca says: beer Ichnusa,   like Socrates, you makes say   what (it) wants]

(b) 'Francesca dice: "Ichnusa beer, like Socrates, makes you say what it wants"' (T)
[Francesca says: Ichnusa beer, like Socrates, makes you say what it wants]

(a) 'Francesca dit: "La bière Ichnusa, comme Socrate, te   fait   dire ce qu'il veut"' (F)
[Francesca says: beer Ichnusa, like   Socrates, you   makes say what (it) wants]

(b) 'Francesca dit: "Ichnusa beer, like Socrates, makes you say what it wants"' (T)
[Francesca says: Ichnusa beer, like Socrates,   makes you say what it wants]

According to Voltolini (2009: 42), the issue extends beyond distinguishing between use and mention. Tyler Burge's work, *Self-reference and Translation* (1978), provides clear evidence that it is impossible for a translator to retain reference, self-reference, and linguistic meaning. Burge's example of translation into German (1978: 138–9) reveals that selecting one of the various meaning components (reference, self-reference, and linguistic meaning) is imperative instead of optional:

'This sentence begins with a four-letter demonstrative'.

(i) Jener   Satz   fängt mit einem hinweisenden Artikel mit vier
   Buchstaben an.
   [That sentence begins with a   demonstrative article   with four
   letters]

(ii) Dieser   Satz   fängt mit einem hinweisenden Artikel mit sechs
   Buchstaben an.
   [This sentence begins with a   demonstrative article   with six
   letters]

(iii) Dieser Satz   fängt mit einem hinweisenden Artikel mit vier
   Buchstaben an.
   [This sentence begins with a   demonstrative article   with four
   letters]

The translator will likely choose one of these alternatives, based on extralinguistic contextual factors. Indeed, according to Burge, a high-quality translation must be 'responsible for preserving certain *global* characteristics of discourse, as well as more *local* features. One cannot always read off the best translation of a sentence (at an occurrence) simply by understanding the sentence itself' (Burge, 1978: 142, italics added).

Despite the fact that it is a matter of principle in translations that not all aspects of meaning can be preserved, Voltolini's conclusions are not overly concerning:

> One can try to argue that if problems of translation arise (and often cannot fail to arise) with respect to an original, in which it is necessary to choose among different factors that contribute to the general signification of the original, which ones to preserve in the translation, then the nuances of meaning indicated by these factors are genuine semantic nuances, not nuances postulated by a theory or some pre-theoretical intuition. Or, conversely, if such nuances are not genuine semantic nuances, then there is no problem of choosing among such nuances in the translation. (Voltolini, 2009: 44)

In the latest case, the phenomena in the original are pragmatic and remain unaffected by translation. As an illustration, Voltolini (2009: 38) presented an instance of irony:

'Ecco   il   re di Sardegna!'
[Here (is) the king of Sardinia!]

   that can be maintained through translation into French (i) and German (ii):

(i) Voilà le   roi de Sardaigne!
    [Here (is) the king of Sardinia!]

(ii) Hier ist der   König von Sardinien!
    [Here (is) the   king of   Sardinia!]

There is no actual object as a king in Sardinia, thus the referential reading of the definite description is not satisfied, but the attributive reading is ironically satisfied by whoever feels like a king in Sardinia.

9 The Translation of Explicit Meaning in Literalism versus Contextualism

Kripke (1979) asserted that explanations of referential-attributive uses of definite descriptions that rely on pragmatics would be too similar to his Gricean explanation, which would 'render any assumptions of distinct senses implausible and superfluous' (Kripke, 1979: 26, fn. 29). Although the Gricean explanation is still valid in the strengthened version of the 'translation test' (Voltolini, 2009), nowadays other explanations based on pragmatics exist to clarify situations where different words are used to encode definite descriptions for referential or attributive purposes.

Indeed, the legacy of Grice is currently being contested by two theoretical projects: the neo-Gricean project or *Literalism*, represented by theorists such as Jay Atlas (1989, 2005), Gerald Gazdar (1979), Robert Harnish (1993), Laurence Horn (1989), and Stephen Levinson (1983, 2000), and the post-Gricean project or *Contextualism*, represented by François Récanati (2004, 2010), Charles Travis (2001, 2008), and particularly by the relevance scholars Dan Sperber and Deirdre Wilson (1986/1995, 2012).

Recanati (2004) defined *Proto-Literalism* as the idea that the literal meaning of a sentence can be ascertained without considering the context in which it is expressed. The philosophers of ideal language who applied a model meant for formalized languages to the theory of meaning regarded sensitivity to context as a shortcoming of natural languages rather than a strength (see Sections 1 and 2). However, natural languages are abundant in indexical elements, which means that sentences in these languages may vary in terms of truth conditions. From a theoretical perspective, the literal meaning of such sentences is linked to the circumstances, and indexicality plays an essential role.

Grice's stance can instead be reconciled with the theses of *Literalism*, which suggests that the determination of a sentence's literal meaning stems from the actions of saturation and disambiguation, commencing from a proposition scheme that aligns with the conventional meaning of the statement (i.e., *minimal proposition*). By means of saturation, the sentence's elements that are closely linked to the context (such as pronouns and verb tenses) are assigned a reference. Through disambiguation, homonymous terms that are phonetically identical but have distinct meanings, such as 'credenza', which can refer to either belief or a kitchen cupboard depending on the context, are given a particular meaning.

Thus, Grice (1989) introduced a level of meaning, known as the level of *what is explicitly said*, which is distinct from both the level of *what is linguistically encoded* (i.e., conventional meaning) and from *what is implicitly communicated* (i.e., implicatures) (see Section 7). According to Grice (1989), the explicit meaning of a sentence is largely determined by its conventional meaning, while inferential processes only intervene to identify references (saturation) and eliminate ambiguities (disambiguation). Linguistic rules dictate the sentence's content in the context, which must be differentiated from the *speaker's meaning*, a pragmatic notion affected by the speaker's beliefs and intentions.[12] Therefore, conversational maxims only apply to the implicit meaning of a sentence, that is, the level of what is implicitly communicated (Bianchi, 2009).

Some authors, such as Kent Bach (1994), argue that pragmatic processes play a role in determining explicit meaning, introducing an additional level of meaning (i.e., *maximal proposition*) derived from the minimal proposition by deriving generalized implicatures. This level of meaning leads to implicit meaning through the derivation of particularized implicatures. However, contextualists find the distinction between minimal and maximal proposition misleading. They believe that the minimal proposition does not align with the natural understanding of speakers regarding what is explicitly said (Carston, 2002).

On the one hand, according to Literalism, there is a literal meaning, determined by the conventional meaning of words and the rules of composition of meanings (*semantics*). On the other hand, Contextualism posits that there is no literal meaning; the explicit level of what is said is largely dependent on contextual information and requires inferential processes that exploit contextual information (*pragmatics*) (Recanati, 2005).

Contextualism is the successor to the school of thought that embraces the 'second' Wittgenstein (1953), Austin (1962), Sellars (1980), as well as the 'second' Davidson (1986). Contextualists hold that literal meaning cannot be properly identified with conventional meaning and maintain that the notion of convention is not essential in a general explanation of linguistic communication. Once the literal meaning is distinguished from the conventional one, it will coincide with what speakers intend to say in a particular communicative situation. Contextualism advocates for the importance of pragmatic effects on the literal content expressed by utterances. Thus, the role of pragmatics is not

---

[12] The speaker aims to produce a certain effect on the listener through the listener's recognition of the speaker's communicative intention. In Grice (1989), the beliefs of the speaker are central for recognizing communicative intention; other scholars have emphasized the role of the listener's beliefs and intentions as well (see Levinson, 1983).

confined to the realm of conversational implicatures, but also enters the realm of what is explicitly said, which was previously reserved for semantic processes only.

In the relevance-theoretic framework, Robyn Carston (2002) proposed two different pragmatic domains, namely *explicatures*, which refer to explicit meaning, and *implicatures*, which refer to implicit meaning. The content of an implicature are determined solely through pragmatic inference, while an explicature is a result of the pragmatic elaboration of a logical form, that is, the semantic representation conveyed by the utterance, and is sourced from both the context and linguistic expressions. Both explicatures and implicatures are considered as communicated assumptions based on the definitions provided by Sperber and Wilson (1986/1995: 182, italics added):

> (I) An assumption communicated by an utterance U is *explicit* [hence an 'explicature'] if and only if it is a development of a logical form encoded by U. [Note: in cases of ambiguity, a surface form encodes more than one logical form, hence the use of the indefinite here, '*a* logical form encoded by U'.]
>
> (II) An assumption communicated by U which is not explicit is *implicit* [hence an 'implicature'].

According to this theoretical viewpoint, the development of the linguistically encoded logical form does not only serve the purpose of resolving ambiguity but also encompasses multiple pragmatic procedures (such as saturation, enrichment, and transfer) in the creation of the explicit meaning level.

Wilson & Carston (2007) suggested a unified explanation for lexical pragmatics, which involves two pragmatic processes of lexical modulation: *broadening* and *narrowing*, which are the outcome of a 'single interpretive process which fine-tunes the interpretation of almost every word' (Wilson & Carston, 2007: 231). These processes involve taking the concepts encoded in the words of an utterance and modifying them into ad hoc *concepts* during the interpretation stage. For instance, in the utterance 'Fiona never drinks when she drives', the word 'drink' is pragmatically narrowed down to a specific part of the concept it encodes, namely 'drink alcohol', to convey the appropriate communicated proposition in the given context. Instead, when uttering the sentence 'My room is rectangular', the concept of 'rectangular' is broadened to the ad hoc concept 'rectangularish', as it is somehow shaped as a rectangle. Also, in utterances featuring figures of speech, such as metaphors like 'Iraida is an angel', a pragmatic enrichment process takes the concept ANGEL and produces an ad hoc concept ANGEL* which attributes the relevant properties to Iraida, such as 'good' and 'empathetic'.

Recanati (1993: 286–7) argues that all these pragmatic processes can gener-ate 'pragmatic ambiguity', that is, 'a form of "ambiguity" which affects truth-conditions even though it is pragmatic (in the sense of contextual) rather than semantic'. According to Recanati (1993, 2004), pragmatic factors extend beyond the speaker's intended meaning that can be understood through infer-ential processes. The context in which the words are used can also influence the meaning of an utterance and alter its truth value.

From this perspective, translation may offer alternative analyses of the original sentences in both cases of semantic and pragmatic ambiguity, as pragmatic processes could carry out the proposition expressed. Looking at translation from this angle, it becomes clear that it does not just help resolve semantic ambiguity by dealing with homonyms (words with multiple unrelated meanings that may require disambiguation in another language), but it also accounts for cases of *sense generality* (Carston, 2002), where a word can have two or more related meanings that may be specifically expressed by another language. In these situations, transla-tion reveals multiple interpretive options to be considered (Van der Sandt, 1988; Atlas, 1989). Indeed, as Jay Atlas (1989: 31) pointed out, 'the sense-generality of a sentence radically underdetermines ... the truth-conditional content of its utterances'; therefore, we must rely on pragmatically inferred aspects of truth-conditional content.

Translation could serve as a means of testing to differentiate between the explicit and implicit facets of communicated content in the field of pragmatics (Ervas, 2022). As pointed out (Falkum, 2007: 120):

> Depending on the interplay between pragmatic inferences and the linguistic resources of the target language, a translator may choose to render an under-specified concept encoded in a source text by a word that more closely encodes the interpretation given to the concept in question. On such an occasion the semantics/pragmatics distinction may be made explicit in the relation between source and target text, in that the target text may (semantic-ally) encode a concept that has been (pragmatically) derived from the concept encoded in the source text. This is not to claim, however, that there exists a single relationship between source and target text in this respect, only that this is one of many relations that may hold between them; one that may give us some insights into the pragmatic inferences made by a translator in the course of translation.

When translating a sentence into another language, the translator may need to decide between various interpretations to develop the logical form (Gutt, 1991). What is crucial to translation as regards enrichment is that languages differ in the strategies used to make meaning explicit. Thus, one language may be equipped to encode very subtle nuances by means of specific linguistic devices, whilst another language may commonly express the equivalent nuances by linguistic devices which encode very vague semantic constraints on the inter-pretation (Ervas, 2014). This forces translators to resort to pragmatic enrich-ment of the logical form to derive the intended meaning of the source sentence.

For example, languages exist that encode what Donnellan referred to as 'pragmatic ambiguity', which relates to the referential versus attributive inter-pretations of definite descriptions. Contrary to Kripke's beliefs (see Section 8), languages with the ability to distinguish between referential and attributive uses of definite descriptions have been found in Northern Frisian (Ebert, 1970), Malagasy (Keenan & Ebert 1973), and Greek (Longobardi, 2005; Guardiano, 2012). Talmy Givón (1978: 251–2) also provided examples of languages that distinguish between different 'degrees of definiteness' using different articles, such as 'di' and 'a', which both translate to 'the', as in the following translations into Frisian:

> Mary was surprised that *the* man who won was drunk.
> (i) Mary wonert ham dat *di* maan wat woon bisööben wiar.
>   [Mary wonder him that *the* man whowon drunk   was]
> (ii) Mary wonert ham dat *a*   maan wat woon bisööben wiar.
>   [Mary wonder him that *the* man whowon drunk   was]

The definite article 'di' can be interpreted as either referential or attributive, while the indefinite article 'a' has an attributive interpretation. In the following translations of 'the' into Malagasy, the article 'ny' allows for both the referential and attributive readings, whereas the article 'ilay' only allows for referential reading:

> Mary was surprised that *the* winner was drunk.
> (i) Gaga Mary fa   mamo *ny* mpandresy.
> [Surprised Mary that drunk *the* winner]
> (ii) Gaga Mary fa   mamo *ilay* mpandresy.
> [Surprised Mary that drunk *the* winner]

These examples show that languages can use various lexical resources to enrich meaning in translation, offering different interpretive possibilities that make mean-ing explicit in the target language (Sequeiros, 2002). Looking at it from this angle, the use of definite descriptions can be most accurately comprehended as a distinct form of enrichment of the logical form encoded by the linguistic utterance (Rouchota, 1992). This is based on the contextual analysis of the definite descrip-tion in its source sentence in either a referential or an attributive way.

As pointed out (Ervas, 2022), translators often have to choose between multiple alternative translations, even when dealing with linguistic phenomena related to what is said in figurative language (Carston, 2002, 2010). For example, with the conventional metaphor 'un abbozzo di sorriso' in Italian ('a sketch of a smile'), the translator may not be able to preserve both the literal and figurative meanings at the same time and must choose between a translation into English that maintains pragmatic equivalence ('a ghost of a smile') or semantic equivalence ('a hint of a smile') (see Section 6).

Sometimes, in order to ensure that the implicature is properly conveyed, a translation may need to employ pragmatic processes such as lexical modulation or enrichment (Carston, 2002; Recanati, 2004, 2010). These processes may 'intrude' into the semantic realm and involve completing the logical form, to arrive at the proposition that is being communicated, and make it explicit in the target language. Indeed, 'the logical form of a linguistic expression seldom, if ever, determines a truth condition, so that pragmatics is inevitably required in the recovery of a fully propositional representation' (Carston, 2002: 184).

Though different, explicatures and implicatures are interconnected: indeed, 'the implicatures of an utterance must be deducible from its explicatures' (Wilson & Carston, 2007: 242), based on relevant contextual assumptions. For instance, consider the following conversational particularized implicature:

> A: Is Andrea superstitious?
> B: She never leaves home on Friday 13th ...
>
> implicating that Andrea is superstitious.

To preserve the implicature, the translator needs to identify a pragmatic equivalent of 'Friday 13th' in the target language, that is, the pragmatic equivalent that works as 'the unlucky day' in the target cultural context (for instance 'venerdì 17' in Italian, 'martes 13' in Spanish) (Ervas, 2014, 2022):

> A: Andrea è superstiziosa? // ¿Andrea es supersticiosa?
> [Andrea is superstitious?]   [Andrea is superstitious?]
> B: Non esce mai di casa il venerdì 17 ...
>   [(She)   never leaves home on Friday 17th ...]
>   // Nunca sale de casa el martes 13 ...
>   //[(She) never leaves home on Tuesady 13th ...]

In other words, the translator must first find the implicit meaning of 'Friday 13th' (i.e., the unlucky day) to correctly derive the implicature in the target language (that Andrea is superstitious). Otherwise, if the translator preserves only the semantic equivalence through a literal translation of the linguistic meaning (for instance 'venerdì 13' in Italian, 'viernes 13' in Spanish), the implicature may be lost in the target cultural context, as in the following example:

A: Andrea è superstiziosa? // ¿Andrea es supersticiosa?

[Andrea is superstitious?]   [Andrea is superstitious?]

B: Non esce mai di casa il venerdì 13 … // Nunca sale de casa el
viernes 13 …

[(She) never leaves home on Friday 13th …]// [(She) never leaves
home on Friday 13th …]

In both translations into Italian and Spanish the implicature (that Andrea actually is superstitious) is lost, because Friday 13th is not considered an unlucky day in those cultural contexts. The translator may choose to explicitly state in the target text or add in a footnote that Andrea is superstitious, but this would be a new proposition resulting from a global pragmatic process rather than a local enrichment of the logical form. Indeed, as the explicature arises from the linguistically encoded logical form of the sentence, the process of mutual adjustment between explicatures and implicatures prevents the inclusion of entire additional propositions into the proposition that is expressed. As remarked (Hall, 2008: 445), 'since such enrichments, which have global effects, are excluded, it follows that free enrichment is essentially local'. This means that it only affects specific parts of a proposition by replacing encoded concepts with inferred concepts or adding material to alter the interpretation of some encoded element, such as making it more specific or broadening its meaning. Thus, the local processes of enrichment are necessary to ensure the implicature of the source sentence in the target language (Ervas, 2022).

Conclusion

The problem of translation has been central within analytic philosophy, from the early philosophers of ideal language and philosophers of ordinary language to contemporary analytic philosophers, as showed in this Element. Nowadays, the philosophical problem of translation is still the topic of lively debates, including in comparison to the 'continental' philosophy of language (Ervas, 2012; Large, 2022). Different trends of research, according to the various areas of interest in analytic philosophy, are beginning to reveal new and promising directions for philosophical inquiry in translation.

One area of research that is currently flourishing concerns the problem of translation within *logical pluralism*, which refers to the numerous non-classical logics that either expand upon or compete with classical logic (Ervas et al., 2019), going beyond the Davidsonian use of the standard first-order quantification theory (see Section 4). Logical pluralism and translations of logics are at the forefront of current debates surrounding the philosophical foundations of *logical consequence* (e.g., Beall & Restall, 2006; Field, 2009; Carnielli et al., 2009). There exist translation-based approaches to the concept of deductive equivalence between consequence relations, that is, relations between sets of sentences (see Section 1). These approaches enable us to compare consequence relations across various languages or systems with distinct data types (such as formulas, sequents, and equations) (French, 2019).

The debate also concerns the problem of understanding which translations of logic preserve the *meaning of logical constants*. Quine (1986) presented the meaning variance argument: when there is a change in logic, it is generally assumed that the meanings of the connectives also change. This has led to concerns regarding the legitimacy of competition between different logics and also raises doubt on the claim that homophonic translation manuals (used for translating a language into itself) maintain meaning. Some scholars (e.g., Shapiro, 2014, 2019) expound on a context-sensitive solution to the question of whether there can exist substantial disagreement between different logics. Other scholars (Kouri, 2019) offer new interpretations of Carnapian pluralism, by separating it from pluralists that rely on meaning variance.

The Gricean perspective on speaker's meaning suggests that the 'logic of conversation' (Grice, 1989) is necessary to understand implicatures and other implicit language uses, instead of relying solely on formal logic. However, it is questioned whether alternative logics could provide a more comprehensive explanation of the translation of the speaker's meaning (Villalonga, 2019). The Gricean logic of conversation and logical pluralism could work hand in hand, arguing that the disagreement between classical and relevant logic is due to two different understandings of logical consequence. These understandings stem from formalizations of logical vocabulary, which are equally legitimate: standard in classical logic and 'pragmatically enriched' in relevant logic (Read, 1988).

Another flourishing area of research, where the problem of translation is becoming more and more relevant, is *conceptual engineering*. Conceptual engineering in philosophy refers to a process of assessing and refining concepts or language use to improve philosophical discussions, debates, and arguments (Cappelen & Plunkett, 2020; Isaac et al., 2022). It involves critically examining the meanings and applications of concepts, identifying potential problems or limitations, across languages, and proposing alternative or modified versions that may better serve philosophical purposes.

The goal of conceptual engineering is to improve our understanding of the world, enhance our ability to communicate and think clearly, and develop more sophisticated and nuanced philosophical theories. Translation may contribute to this goal by acting as a litmus test for conceptual differences across languages, which can be valuable for improving our own conceptual system. As the resources we have for translation can be insufficient due to gaps in expressions or unnecessary information, a range of strategies – from minor linguistic improvements to radical reorganization – can be proposed by drawing on ideas from conceptual engineering (Bariselli & Sawyer, 2021).

Also, the theme of *linguistic injustice* in the Anglophone tradition of analytic philosophy has been a central topic of heated debate (Contesi & Terrone, 2018). It refers to the unfair treatment or marginalization of certain languages, which can lead to the exclusion of specific groups from philosophical discourse. This concept suggests that languages other than English are considered to be 'less prestigious' in analytic philosophy and are often overlooked in philosophical academia, leading to the perpetuation of biases, already criticized in the literature (Hacking, 1975, 1986, and Section 5), and limiting the diversity of perspectives in philosophical discussions. After all, the 'founding fathers' of analytic philosophy themselves wrote in languages other than English (e.g., Frege, Carnap, and Wittgenstein wrote in German, Tarski in Polish) and were translated into English by other analytic philosophers (e.g., Austin translated Frege, Anscombe translated Wittgenstein).

Some scholars even pointed at linguistic injustice as an internal problem possibly causing the decadence of analytic philosophy (Contesi et al., 2022), because of linguistic imperialism that overshadows the contributions that can come from another linguistic-cultural context, possibly enriching and bringing vital drive to the analytic-philosophical debate. Other scholars argued that simply being at a comparative disadvantage to others does not constitute a legitimate injustice as long as essential civil, political, and social measures are established (Chiesa & Galeotti, 2018). However, as already remarked (Schliesser, 2018), the presence of philosophical translator-advocates seems anyway necessary to overcome the limitations caused by the restricted language usage in the field of analytic philosophy. The philosophical translator-advocates recognize that lack of translation or bad translation is a huge epistemic cost: English as a *lingua franca* is not a negligible linguistic barrier in analytic philosophy, as philosophical concepts themselves are inextricably linked to the language they are encoded in. Thus, translation still highlights the need for greater recognition of conceptual differences which are fundamental for the life of analytic philosophy itself and encourages the inclusion of non-dominant languages in analytic-philosophical discourse.

References

Arrojo, R. (2010). 'Philosophy and Translation'. In *Handbook of Translation Studies*. Yves Gambier and Luc van Doorslaer (eds.). Amsterdam: John Benjamins: 247–51.

Atlas, J. (1989). *Philosophy without Ambiguity*. Oxford: Clarendon Press.

Atlas, J. D. (2005). *Logic, Meaning and Conversation: Semantical Underdeterminacy, Implicature, and Their Interface*. Oxford: Oxford University Press.

Austin, J. L. (1962). *How to Do Things with Words*. Oxford: Oxford University Press.

Avramides, A. (1989). *Meaning and Mind: An Examination of a Gricean Account of Language*. Cambridge: The MIT Press.

Bach, K. (1994). 'Conversational Impliciture'. *Mind & Language* 9(2): 124–62.

Baker, M. (1992). *In Other Words: A Coursebook on Translation*. London: Routledge.

Bariselli, M. and Fisher, S. (2021). 'Not Just Words: Balancing Efficiency and Integrity in Translation'. Talk at the online Symposium *Philosophy in/on Translation* (9–10 September 2021).

Bassnett, S. (2013). 'Postcolonialism and/as Translation'. In *The Oxford Handbook of Postcolonial Studies*. Graham Huggan (ed.). Oxford: Oxford University Press: 340–58.

Beall, J. C. and Restall, G. (2006). *Logical Pluralism*. Oxford: Clarendon Press.

Bianchi, C. (2009). *Pragmatica cognitiva: I meccanismi della comunicazione*. Roma: Laterza.

Boghossian, P. A. (1997). 'Analyticity'. In *A Companion to the Philosophy of Language*. Bob Hale, Crispin Wright, and Alexander Miller (eds.). Cambridge: Blackwell: 578–618.

Burge, T. (1973). 'Reference and Proper Names'. *Journal of Philosophy* 70(14): 425–29.

Burge, T. (1978). 'Self–Reference and Translation'. In *Meaning and Translation*. Guenthner, F. and Guenthner–Reutter, M. (eds.), London: Duckworth: 137–53.

Burgess, J. P. (2005). 'Translating Names'. *Analysis* 65(287): 196–205.

Cappelen, H. and Plunkett,D. (2020). 'Introduction: A Guided Tour of Conceptual Engineering and Conceptual Ethics'. In *Conceptual Engineering and Conceptual Ethics*. Alexis Burgess, Herman Cappelen, and David Plunkett (eds.). Oxford: Oxford Academic: 1–34.

Carnap, R. (1934). *Logische Syntax der Sprache*. Wien: Springer; *The Logical Syntax of Language*. Amethe Smeaton (trans.). London: Routledge, 1937.

Carnap, R. (1942). *Introduction to Semantics*. Cambridge, MA: Harvard University Press.

Carnap, R. (1947). *Meaning and Necessity: A Study in Semantics and Modal Logic*. Chicago: University of Chicago Press.

Carnap, R. (1955). 'Meaning and Synonymy in Natural Languages'. *Philosophical Studies* **6**(3); reprinted in *Meaning and Necessity*. Chicago: Chicago University Press, 1956: 233–47.

Carnielli, W. A., Coniglio, M. E., and D'Ottaviano, I. M. L. (2009). 'New Ddimensions on Translations between Logics'. *Logica Universalis* **3**(1): 1–18.

Carston, R. (2002). *Thoughts and Utterances: The Pragmatics of Explicit Communication*. Oxford: Blackwell.

Carston, R. (2010). 'Metaphor: Ad Hoc Concepts, Literal Meaning and Mental Images'. *Proceedings of the Aristotelian Society* **110**(3): 295–321.

Catford, J. C. (1965). *A Linguistic Theory of Translation: An Essay on Applied Linguistics*. London: Oxford University Press.

Chesterman, A. (1989). *Memes of Translation*. Amsterdam: John Benjamins.

Chiesa, F. and Galeotti, A. E. (2018). 'Linguistic Justice and Analytic Philosophy'. *Philosophical Papers* **47**(1): 155–82.

Contesi, F. and Terrone, E. (2018). '"Introduction" to Linguistic Justice and Analytic Philosophy'. *Philosophical Papers* **47**(1):1–20.

Contesi, F., Chapman, L., and Sandis, C. (2022). 'Analytic Philosophy Has a Language Problem: The Roots of Its Contemporary Decadence'. *IAI News*, 7 April.

D'Agostini, F. (1997). *Analitici e continentali: guida alla filosofia degli ultimi trent'anni*. Milano: Cortina.

Davidson D. (1967). 'Truth and Meaning' *Synthese* 17: 304–23. Reprinted in *Inquiries into Truth and Interpretation*, Oxford: Clarendon Press, 1984: 17–36.

Davidson, D. (1973). 'Radical Interpretation'. In *Dialectica* 27: 313–28. Reprinted in *Inquiries into Truth and Interpretation*, Oxford: Clarendon Press, 1984: 125–40.

Davidson, D. (1974). 'On the Very Idea of a Conceptual Scheme'. In *Proceedings and Addresses of the American Philosophical Association* 47: 5–20; Reprinted in *Inquiries into Truth and Interpretation*, Oxford: Clarendon Press, 1984: 183–98.

Davidson, D. (1980a). *Essays on Action and Events*. Oxford: Clarendon Press.

Davidson, D. (1980b). 'Mental Events'. In *Essays on Action and Events*. Oxford: Clarendon Press: 207–25.

Davidson, D. (1984a). *Inquiries into Truth and Interpretation*. Oxford: Clarendon Press.

Davidson, D. (1984b). 'Introduction'. In *Inquiries into Truth and Interpretation*. Oxford: Clarendon Press: xiii -xx.

Davidson, D. (1984c). 'Truth and Meaning'. In *Inquiries into Truth and Interpretation*. Oxford: Clarendon Press: 17–36.

Davidson, D. (1984d). 'Radical Interpretation'. In *Inquiries into Truth and Interpretation*. Oxford: Clarendon Press: 125–39.

Davidson, D. (1984e). 'Belief and the Basis of Meaning'. In *Inquiries into Truth and Interpretation*. Oxford: Clarendon Press: 141–54.

Davidson, D. (1984f). 'On the Very Idea of a Conceptual Scheme'. In *Inquiries Into Truth and Interpretation*. Oxford: Clarendon Press: 183–98.

Davidson, D. (1986). 'A Nice Derangement of Epitaphs'. In *Truth and Interpretation. Perspectives on the Philosophy of Donald Davidson*. Ernie Lepore (ed.). Oxford: Blackwell: 433–46.

Davidson, D. (1989). James Joyce and Humpty Dumpty James Joyce and Humpty Dumpty. In *Proceedings of the Norwegian Academy of Science and Letters*, 54–66; Reprinted in P. French, T. E. Uehling, H. Wettstein (eds.), *Midwest Studies in Philosophy*, vol. xvi, Notre Dame: University of Notre Dame Press, 1991, 1–12.

Davidson, D. (1990). 'The Structure and Content of Truth'. *Journal of Philosophy* **87**(6): 279–328.

Davidson, D. (1991). 'James Joyce and Humpty Dumpty'. In *Midwest Studies in Philosophy*. Peter French, Theodore E. Uehling, and Howard K. Wettstein (eds.). Notre Dame: University of Notre Dame Press: 1–12.

Davidson, D. (1992). 'The Second Person'. In *Midwest Studies in Philosophy*. Peter French, Theodore E. Uehling, and Howard K. Wettstein (eds.). Notre Dame: University of Notre Dame Press: 255–67.

Davidson, D. (1994a). 'Radical Interpretation Interpreted'. *Philosophical Perspectives* **8**: 121–8.

Davidson, D. (1994b). 'The Social Aspect of Language'. In *The Philosophy of Michael Dummett*. Brian McGuinness and Gianluigi Oliveri (eds.). Dordrecht: Kluwer: 1–16.

Davidson, D. (1997). 'Seeing through Language'. In *Thought and Language*. John Preston (ed.). New York: Cambridge University Press: 15–27.

Devitt, M. (1984). *Realism and Truth*. Princeton: Princeton University Press.

Donnellan, K. (1966). 'Reference and Definite Descriptions'. *The Philosophical Review* **75**(3): 281–304.

Duhem, P. (1906). *La théorie physique, son objet et sa structure*. Paris: Chevalier et Rivière.

Dummett, M. (1978). *Truth and Other Enigmas*. Cambridge, MA: Harvard University Press.

Dummett, M. (1986). 'A Nice Derangement of Epitaphs: Some Comments on Davidson and Hacking'. In *Truth and Interpretation: Perspectives on the Philosophy of Donald Davidson*. Ernie Lepore (ed.). Oxford: Blackwell: 459–76.

Ebert, K. (1970). *Referenz, Sprechsituation und die bestimmten Artikel in einem norderfriesischen Dialekt* [PhD Dissertation]. Kiel: Universität Kiel.

Ervas, F. (2008). *Uguale ma diverso. Il mito dell'equivalenza nella traduzione*. Macerata: Quodlibet.

Ervas, F. (2012). 'The Definition of Translation in Davidson's Philosophy: Semantic Equivalence versus Functional Equivalence'. *Traduction, Terminologie, Rédaction* **25**(1): 243–65.

Ervas, F. (2014). 'On Semantic and Pragmatic Equivalence in Translation'. In *Translating the DCFR and Drafting the CESL: A Pragmatic Perspective*. Barbara Pasa and Lucia Morra (eds.). Munich: Sellier: 87–101.

Ervas, F. (2022). 'Translation as a Test for the Explicit-Implicit Distinction'. *The Journal for the Philosophy of Language, Mind and the Arts* **3**(2): 249–66.

Ervas, F. and Morra, L. (2013). 'Traduzione'. *Analytical and Philosophical Explanation* **8**(2): 146–80.

Ervas, F., Ledda, A., Paoli, F., and Sergioli, G. (2019). 'Introduction: Logical Pluralism and Translation'. *Topoi* **38**(2): 263–4.

Falkum, I. L. (2007). 'A Relevance-Theoretic Analysis of Concept Narrowing and Broadening in English and Norwegian Original Texts and Translations'. *Languages in Contrast* **7**(2): 119–41.

Field, H. (2009). 'Pluralism in Logic'. *The Review of Symbolic Logic* **2**(2): 342–59.

Felappi, G. and Santambrogio, M. (2019). 'Lost in Translation?' *Topoi* **38**(2): 265–76.

Fodor, J. and Lepore, E. (1992). *Holism: A Shopper's Guide*. Oxford: Blackwell.

Frege, G. (1879–1891). 'Logik'. In *Nachgelassene Schriften*. Hans Hermes, Friedrich Kambartel, and Friedrich Kaulbach (eds.). Hamburg: Felix Meiner: 1–8; 'Logic'. Peter Long and Roger M. White (trans.). In *Posthumous Writings*. Oxford: Blackwell, 1979: 1–8.

Frege, G. (1884). *Die Grundlagen der Arithmetik. Eine logisch-mathematische Untersuchung über den Begriff der Zahl*. Breslau: Verlag; *Foundations of*

Arithmetic: A Logico-Mathematical Enquiry into the Concept of Number. John Austin (trans.). Evanston: Northwestern University Press, 1950.

Frege, G. (1892). 'Über Sinn und Bedeutung. Zeitschrift für Philosophie und philosophische'. Kritik **100**(1): 25–50; 'On Sense and Reference'. Max Black (trans.). In *Meaning and Reference*. Adrian W. Moore (ed.). Oxford: Oxford University Press, 1993: 23–42.

French, R. (2019). 'Notational Variance and Its Variants'. *Topoi* **38**(2): 321–31.

Gazdar, G. (1979). *Pragmatics: Implicature, Presupposition, and Logical Form*. New York: Academic Press.

Givón, T. (1978). 'Universal Grammar, Lexical Structure and Translatability'. In *Meaning and Translation: Philosophical and Linguistic Approaches*. Franz Guenthner and Monica Guenthner-Reutter (eds.). London: Duckworth: 235–72.

Glock, H.-J. (2007). 'Relativism, Commensurability and Translatability'. *Ratio* **20**(4): 377–402.

Glock, H.-J. (2008). *What Is Analytic Philosophy?* Cambridge: Cambridge University Press.

Grandy, R. E. (1973). 'Reference, Meaning and Belief'. *Journal of Philosophy* **70**(14): 439–52.

Grice, H. P. (1975). 'Logic and Conversation'. In *Syntax and Semantics: Vol. 3, Speech Acts*. Peter Cole and Jerry Morgan (eds.). New York: Academic Press: 41–58.

Grice, H. P. (1989). *Studies in the Way of Words*. Cambridge, MA: Harvard University Press.

Grice, H. P. (2001). *Aspects of Reason*. Oxford: Clarendon Press.

Grice, H. P. and Strawson, P. F. (1956). 'In Defense of a Dogma'. *The Philosophical Review* **65**(2): 141–58.

Guardiano, C. (2012). 'Parametric Changes in the History of the Greek Article'. In *Grammatical Change: Origins, Nature, Outcomes*. Dianne Jonas, John Witman, and Andrew Garrett (eds.). Oxford: Oxford University Press: 179–97.

Gutt, E. A. (1991). *Translation and Relevance: Cognition and Context*. Oxford: Basil Blackwell.

Hacking, I. (1975). *Why Does Language Matter to Philosophy?* Cambridge: Cambridge University Press.

Hacking, I. (1986). 'The Parody of Conversation'. In *Truth and Interpretation. Perspectives on the Philosophy of Donald Davidson*. Ernie Lepore (ed.). Oxford: Blackwell: 447–58.

Hacking, I. (1999). *The Social Construction of What?* Cambridge, MA: Harvard University Press.

Hall, A. (2008). 'Free Enrichment or Hidden Indexicals?' *Mind & Language* **23** (4): 426–56.

Halverson, S. (1997). 'The Concept of Equivalence in Translation Studies: Much Ado About Something'. *Target* **9**(2): 207–34.

Harman, G. (1975). 'Moral Relativism Defended'. *Philosophical Review* **84**(1): 3–22.

Harnish, R. (1993). *Basic Topics in the Philosophy of Language*. Englewood Cliffs: Prentice-Hall.

Hirst, G. (1987). *Semantic Interpretation and the Resolution of Ambiguity*. Cambridge: Cambridge University Press.

Holdcroft, D. (1981). 'Principles of Conversation, Speech Acts, and Radical Interpretation'. In *Meaning and Understanding*. Herman Parrett and Jacques Bouveresse (eds.). Berlin: De Gruyter: 195–7.

Horn, L. (1989). *A Natural History of Negation*. Chicago: University of Chicago Press.

Horn, L. (2006). *The Handbook of Pragmatics*. Oxford: Blackwell.

Isaac, M. G., Koch, S., and Nefdt, R. (2022). 'Conceptual Engineering: A Road Map to Practice'. *Philosophy Compass* **17**(10), 1–15.

Janik, A. and Toulmin, S. (1973). *Wittgenstein's Vienna*. New York: Simon and Schuster.

Jakobson, R. (1959). 'On Linguistic Aspects of Translation'. In *On Translation*. Reuben A. Brower (ed.). Cambridge, MA: Harvard University Press: 232–9; reprinted in *Selected Writings*. Paris: Mouton, 1971: 260–6.

Kasher, A. (1976). 'Conversational Maxims and Rationality'. In *Language in Focus: Foundations, Methods and Systems*. Asa Kasher (ed.). Dordrecht: Reidel: 197–216.

Katz, J. J. (1978). 'Effability and Translation'. In *Meaning and Translation: Philosophical and Linguistic Approaches*. Franz Guenthner and Monica Guenthner-Reutter (eds.). London: Duckworth: 191–234.

Keenan, E. and Ebert, K. (1973). 'A Note on Marking Transparency and Opacity'. *Linguistic Inquiry* **4**(3): 421–4.

Kenny, D. (1998). 'Equivalence'. In *Routledge Encyclopaedia of Translation Studies*. Mona Baker (ed.). London: Routledge: 77–80.

Koller, W. (1989). 'Equivalence in Translation Theory'. In *Readings in Translation Theory*. Andrew Chesterman (ed.). Helsinki: Finn Lectura: 99–104.

Kouri, T. A. (2019). 'New Interpretation of Carnap's Logical Pluralism'. *Topoi* **38**(2): 305–14.

Kripke, S. (1979). 'Speaker's Reference and Semantic Reference'. In *Contemporary Perspectives in the Philosophy of Language*. Peter French,

Theodore E. Uehling, and Howard K. Wettstein (eds.). Minneapolis: University of Minnesota Press: 6–27.

Kuhn, T. S. (1970). 'Reflections on My Critics'. In *Criticism and the Growth of Knowledge*. Imre Lakatos and Alan Musgrave (eds.). Cambridge: Cambridge University Press.

Large, D. (2014). 'On the Work of Philosopher-Translators'. In *Literary Translation*. Jean Boase-Beier, Antoinette Fawcett, and Philip Wilson (eds.). London: Palgrave Macmillan: 182–203.

Large, D. (2022). 'Translation and Philosophy'. In *The Cambridge Handbook of Translation*. Kirsten Malmkjær (ed.). Cambridge: Cambridge University Press: 258–76.

Leech, G. N. (1983). *Principles of Pragmatics*. London: Longman.

Levinson, S. C. (1983). *Pragmatics*. Cambridge: Cambridge University Press.

Levinson, S. C. (2000). *Presumptive Meanings: The Theory of Generalized Conversational Implicature*. Cambridge: The MIT Press.

Longobardi, G. (2005). 'Toward a Unified Grammar of Reference'. *Zeitschrift für Sprachwissenschaft* **24**(1): 5–44.

Malmkjær, K. (1993). 'Underpinning Translation Theory'. *Target* **5**(2): 133–48.

Malmkjær, K. (1998). 'Analytical Philosophy and Translation'. In *Routledge Encyclopaedia of Translation Studies*. Mona Baker (ed.). London: Routledge: 8–13.

Malmkjær, K. (2005). *Linguistics and the Language of Translation*. Edinburgh: Edinburgh University Press.

Marconi, D. (2010). 'Translatable/Untranslatable'. In *Translation: Transfer, Text and Topic*. Pierluigi Barrotta and Anna L. Lepschy (eds.). Perugia: Guerra Edizioni: 9–13.

Marconi, D. (2019). 'Analysis as Translation'. *Topoi* **38**(2): 347–60.

Mates, B. (1950). *Meaning and Interpretation*. Los Angeles: University of California Press.

Montague, R. (1973). 'The Proper Treatment of Quantification in Ordinary English'. In *Formal Philosophy: Selected Papers of Richard Montague*. New Haven: Yale University Press: 247–70.

Montibeller, M. (2009). 'L'*Übersetzungsregel* in Wittgenstein'. *Paradigmi* **27**(2): 47–58.

Morra, L. (2004). 'Quine, Brower e la traduzione: un carteggio inedito'. *Rivista di filosofia* **95**(2): 247–74.

Morra, L. (2009). 'Traduzione e filosofia analitica: prima di Quine'. *Paradigmi* **27**(2): 17–31.

Oliveira, P., Alois, P., and Arley, M. (2019). *Wittgenstein in/on Translation*. Campinas: Coleção CLE.

Peirce, C. S. (1865). *Writings of Charles S. Peirce: A Chronological Edition.* Bloomington: Indiana University Press, 1982–1989, vol. 1, p. 333

Pym, A. (1992). 'Equivalence Defines Translation'. In *Translation and Text Transfer: An Essay on the Principles of Intercultural Communication.* Frankfurt: Peter Lang: 37–49.

Pym, A. (2007). 'Philosophy and Translation'. In *A Companion to Translation Studies.* Piotr Kuhiwczak and Karin Littau (eds.). Clevedon: Multilingual Matters: 24–44.

Quine, W. V. O. (1951). 'The Problem of Meaning in Linguistics'. In *From a Logical Point of View.* Cambridge, MA: Harvard University Press: 47–64.

Quine, W. V. O. (1953). 'Two Dogmas of Empiricism'. In *From a Logical Point of View.* Cambridge, MA: Harvard University Press: 20–46.

Quine, W. V. O. (1959). 'Meaning and Translation'. In *On Translation.* Reuben A. Brower (ed.). Cambridge, MA: Harvard University Press: 148–72; reprinted in *The Structure of Language. Readings in Philosophy of Language.* Jerry A. Fodor and Jerrold J. Katz (eds.). Egelwood Cliffs: Prentice-Hall, 1964: 460–78.

Quine, W. V. O. (1960). *Word and Object.* Cambridge: The MIT Press.

Quine W.V.O. (1968). 'Ontological Relativity'. *Journal of Philosophy* 65 (7):185–212.

Quine, W. V. O. (1969a). 'Ontological Relativity'. In *Ontological Relativity and Other Essays.* New York: Columbia University Press: 26–68.

Quine, W. V. O. (1969b). 'Epistemology Naturalized'. In *Ontological Relativity and Other Essays.* New York: Columbia University Press: 69–90.

Quine, W. V. O. (1986). *Philosophy of Logic.* Cambridge, MA: Harvard University Press.

Rawling, P. (2023). 'Davidson on Indeterminacy and "Passing Theories": Need Translators Worry?' *Perspectives* **31**(1): 119–29.

Read, S. (1988). *Relevant Logic: A Philosophical Examination of Inference.* Oxford: Basil Blackwell.

Recanati,F. (1993). *Direct Reference: From Language to Thought.* Oxford: Basil Blackwell.

Recanati, F. (2004). *Literal Meaning.* Cambridge: Cambridge University Press.

Recanati, F. (2005). 'Literalism and Contextualism: Some Varieties'. In *Contextualism in Philosophy: Knowledge, Meaning, and Truth.* Gerhard Preyer and Georg Peter (eds.). Oxford: Oxford University Press: 171–96.

Recanati, F. (2010). *Truth-Conditional Pragmatics.* Oxford: Oxford University Press.

Reiss, K. and Vermeer, H. (1984). 'Äquivalenz und Adäquatheit'. In *Grundlegung einer allgemeinen Translationstheorie.* Tübingen: Max Niemeyer.

Rouchota, V. (1992). 'On the Referential/Attributive Distinction'. *Lingua* **87**(1–2): 137–67.

Russell, B. (1905). 'On Denoting'. *Mind* **14**(56): 479–93.

Santambrogio, M. (1992). 'W. V. Quine'. In *Introduzione alla filosofia analitica del linguaggio*. Marco Santambrogio (ed.). Roma-Bari: Laterza: 179–222.

Santambrogio, M. (2002). 'Belief and Translation'. *Journal of Philosophy* **99** (12): 624–47.

Schlick, M. (1936). 'Meaning and Verification'. *Philosophical Revue* **44**; reprinted in *Readings in Philosophical Analysis*. Herbert Feigl and Wilfrid Sellars (eds.). New York: Appleton Century Crofts, 1949: 146–70.

Schliesser, E. (2018). 'On Philosophical Translator-Advocates and Linguistic Injustice'. *Philosophical Papers* **47**(1): 93–121.

Searle, J. (1969). *Speech Acts: An Essay in the Philosophy of Language*. Cambridge: Cambridge University Press.

Searle, J. (1993). 'Metaphor'. In *Metaphor and Thought*. Andrew Ortony (ed.). Cambridge: Cambridge University Press: 83–111.

Sellars, W. (1963). 'Truth and Correspondence'. In *Science, Perception and Reality*. London: Routledge and Kegan Paul: 197–224.

Sellars, W. (1980). *Pure Pragmatics and Possible Worlds: The Early Essays of Wilfrid Sellars*, edited and introduced by J. Sicha, Reseda: Ridgeview.

Sequeiros, X. R. (2002). 'Interlingual Pragmatic Enrichment in Translation'. *Journal of Pragmatics* **34**(8): 1069–89.

Shapiro, S. (2014). *Varieties of Logic*. Oxford: Oxford University Press.

Shapiro, S. (2019). 'Translating Logical Terms'. *Topoi* **38**(2): 291–303.

Sperber, D. and Wilson, D. (1986/1995). *Relevance Theory: Communication and Cognition*. Oxford: Blackwell.

Sperber, D. and Wilson, D. (2012). *Meaning and Relevance*. Cambridge: Cambridge University Press.

Stern, J. (2006). 'Metaphor, Literal, Literalism'. *Mind and Language* **21**(3): 243–79.

Tarski, A. (1933). 'Pojecie prawdy w jezykach nauk dedukcyjnych'. *Prace Towarzystwa Naukowego Warszawskiego*, Wydzial III Nauk. Matematyczno-Fizycznych **34**(13): 172–98; 'The Concept of truth in Formalized Languages'. In *Logic, Semantics, Metamathematics*. Joseph H. Woodger (trans.). Oxford: Clarendon Press: 152–278.

Tarski, A. (1944). 'The Semantic Conception of Truth'. Philosophy and Phenomenological Research **4**(3): 341–76; reprinted in *Collected Papers*. Steven R. Givant and Ralph N. Mackenzie (eds.). Basel: Birkhauser, vol. 2: 665–99.

Travis, C. (2001). *The Uses of Sense: Wittgenstein's Philosophy of Language*. Oxford: Oxford University Press.

Travis, C. (2008). *Occasion Sensitivity: Selected Essays*. Oxford: Oxford University Press.

Van den Broeck, R. (1978). 'The Concept of Equivalence in Translation Theory: Some Critical Reflections'. In *Literature and Translation. New Perspectives in Literary Studies*. James S. Holmes, José Lambert, and Raymond Van den Broeck (eds.). Leuven, Acco: 29–47.

Van der Sandt, R. (1988). *Context and Presupposition*. London: Croom Helm.

Van Leuven-Zwart, K. and Naaijkens, T. (eds.) (1991). *Translation Studies: The State of the Art. Proceedings of the First James S. Holmes Symposium on Translation Studies*. Leiden: Brill.

Villalonga, T. P. (2019). 'From Natural to Formal Language: A Case for Logical Pluralism'. *Topoi* **38**(2): 333–45.

Voltolini, A. (2009). 'L'irrimediabile dilemma del traduttore'. *Paradigmi* **27**(2): 33–46.

Wallace, J. (1972). 'Positive, Comparative, Superlative'. *Journal of Philosophy* **69**(21): 773–82.

Whorf, B. L. (1956). 'The Punctual and Segmentative Aspects of Verbs in Hopi'. In *Language, Thought and Reality: Selected Writings of Benjamin Lee Whorf*. John B. Carroll (ed.). Cambridge: The MIT Press: 51–6.

Wilson, D. and Carston, R. (2007). 'A Unitary Approach to Lexical Pragmatics: Relevance, Inference and Ad hoc Concepts'. In *Advances in Pragmatics*. Noel Burton-Roberts (ed.). Basingstoke: Palgrave: 230–60.

Wilson, P. (2016). *Translation after Wittgenstein*. London: Routledge.

Wittgenstein, L. (1921). *Logisch-philosophische Abhandlung*. In *Annalen der Naturphilosophie*. Wilhelm Ostwald (ed.). Leipzig: Reinhold Berger; *Tractatus logico-philosophicus* (TLP). Frank P. Ramsey and Charles K. Ogden (trans.). London: Routledge & Kegan Paul, 2022.

Wittgenstein, L. (1929–1948). *Zettel*. Bilingual Edition, Gertrude Elizabeth Margaret. Anscombe (trans.). Los Angeles: University of California Press.

Wittgenstein, L. (1953). *Philosophische Untersuchungen*. Frankfurt am Main: Suhrkamp; *Philosophical Investigations* (PI). Gertrude Elizabeth Margaret Anscombe, Peter M. S. Hacker, and Joachim Schulte (trans.). Oxford: Blackwell, 2009.

Zwicky, A. and Sadock, J. (1975). 'Ambiguity Tests and How to Fail Them'. In *Syntax and Semantics*. John Kimball (ed.). New York: Academic Press: 1–36.

Acknowledgements

Throughout my work on translation in analytic philosophy, I have received invaluable feedback from Massimiliano Carrara, Robyn Carston, Andrew Chesterman, Massimo Dell'Utri, Rosaria Egidi, Stefano Gensini, Elisabetta Gola, Luca Illetterati, Bipin Indurkhya, Kirsten Malmkjær, Charles Le Blanc, Pier Luigi Lecis, Josep Macià, Diego Marconi, Marcello Montibeller, Lucia Morra, Pietro Perconti, Luigi Perissinotto, Roberto Pujia, François Recanati, Marco Santambrogio, Marina Sbisà, Zsuzsanna Schnell, Luisa Simonutti, Pietro Storari, Imre Toth, Alberto Voltolini, and two anonymous reviewers for this Element. I am also very grateful to the research groups APhEx (Analytical and Philosophical Explanation), 'ALOPHIS' (Applied LOgic, Philosophy and HIstory of Science, University of Cagliari), and 'Transphil' (Philosophy in/on translation, organized by Alice Leal, University of Vienna, and Philip Wilson, University of East Anglia).

To my children, Ilaria and Leonardo

Cambridge Elements ☰

Translation and Interpreting

The series is edited by Kirsten Malmkjær with Sabine Braun as associate editor for Elements focusing on Interpreting.

Kirsten Malmkjær
University of Leicester

Kirsten Malmkjær is Professor Emeritus of Translation Studies at the University of Leicester. She has taught Translation Studies at the universities of Birmingham, Cambridge, Middlesex and Leicester and has written extensively on aspects of both the theory and practice of the discipline. *Translation and Creativity* (London: Routledge) was published in 2020 and *The Cambridge Handbook of Translation*, which she edited, was published in 2022. She is preparing a volume entitled *Introducing Translation* for the Cambridge Introductions to Language and Linguistics series.

Editorial Board

About the Series

Elements in Translation and Interpreting present cutting edge studies on the theory, practice and pedagogy of translation and interpreting. The series also features work on machine learning and AI, and human-machine interaction, exploring how they relate to multilingual societies with varying communication and accessibility needs, as well as text-focused research.

Cambridge Elements $\equiv$

Translation and Interpreting

Elements in the Series

Translation and Genre
B. J. Woodstein

On-Screen Language in Video Games
Mikołaj Deckert, Krzysztof Hejduk

Navigating the Web
Claire Y. Shih

The Graeco-Arabic Translation Movement
El-Hussein A Y Aly

Interpreting as Translanguaging
Lili Han, Zhisheng (Edward) Wen, Alan James Runcieman

Creative Classical Translation
Paschalis Nikolaou

Translation as Creative–Critical Practice
Delphine Grass

Translation in Analytic Philosophy
Francesca Ervas

A full series listing is available at: www.cambridge.org/EITI.

Printed in the USA
CPSIA information can be obtained
at www.ICGtesting.com
CBHW061143091024
15595CB00006B/368